Red Stitches

Red Stitches

The inspiring true story of LeAnn Sanders Shelton and her journey from the dugout of personal tragedy to a mound of victories

LeAnn Sanders Shelton

All rights reserved. No part of this book may be reproduced, stored, or transmitted by any means, whether auditory, graphic, mechanical, or electronic without written permission of both publisher and author, except in the case of brief excerpts used in critical articles and reviews. Unauthorized reproduction of any part of this work is illegal and is punishable by law.

ISBN 1-944662-42-4

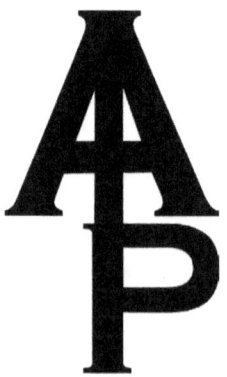

Publishing date: November 2019

Cover Design by Michael Scott, MASgraphicarts.com

Dedication

For my son, Gunner Lake Shelton. Words are simply not enough to express how amazing I feel to have you as my son. You make my life complete. You are my anchor.

I love you!

Mom

"With God nothing is impossible."

Luke 1:37

Contents

Dedication v

1st Inning Family Ties 1

2nd Inning The Lawnmower 13

3rd Inning Adapting to Life with No Arm 27

4th Inning "Mom, I Wanna Play Softball!" 33

Red Stitches Photographs 65

5th Inning Jeremy and Gunner Lake 97

6th Inning A Slice of Heaven and Bethany's Wave 111

7th Inning What Part Are YOU Missing? 129

About the Author 139

Acknowledgements 142

How to Order 153

Foreword

I became involved in girls softball in 1968 when I founded Dixie Girls Softball, later to become Dixie Softball, Inc. in 1975. In the 51 years since, I have been honored with numerous awards (local, state and national). The honors are great, but none compare to the honor of having been a vehicle that allowed thousands upon thousands of girls to play an organized sport (softball).

For too many years, only the boys had organized sports in the South. Dixie Softball is the only girls softball program that is played in multiple states—it has always been and will forever be for the girls.

Of all the personal honors I have received through Dixie Softball, none compare to that day in the summer of 1990 when I was asked to come watch a young player on the Pickens County, Alabama Dixie Softball tournament team. I was not told why I should come watch this young lady, only that I was to come and just watch. What I observed totally amazed me. There was a young girl on the field who had only one arm. To watch her warm up and see how she was able to catch the ball in a glove and then remove the glove and throw the ball with the same arm without missing a beat was fascinating. When she came up to bat I watched her swing that bat with power and run the bases like she was on fire. It was unreal. She roamed the outfield like she owned it. Then she was brought in to pitch. Wow!

This girl was a complete softball player and yet she had only one arm. Her name? LeAnn Sanders. LeAnn went on to become a great softball player for Pickens County High School and was inducted into the Dixie Softball Hall of Fame, and even has an award named in her honor: The LeAnn Sanders Shelton Dixie Softball Courage Award, which is given out annually.

But the greatest thing about LeAnn is what she has accomplished outside of softball. She can do anything she sets her mind to doing. What some would call a "disability" has not stopped her one bit. She is a picture of perseverance, tenacity, and determination. Most of all, LeAnn is a caring person. In November 2015, a tremendous twelve-year-old Dixie Softball pitcher from Sylacauga, Alabama, Heaven Harris, who was headed for a great softball career, lost her pitching arm in a terrible ATV accident. When LeAnn learned of Heaven's accident she jumped in immediately and offered her knowledge and skill as a one-armed softball player—she worked with her and before long Heaven was back playing softball in the spring of 2016, making her school team and thriving as a player.

All I know is that LeAnn has been a big influence on me and many others in the game of softball. I am proud of what she has accomplished as a young softball player but more so as an adult. God bless LeAnn Sanders Shelton. She is an inspiration to us all! Enjoy the book; I know I will.

What is the greatest honor I have ever had bestowed upon me in my 51 years of girls softball? It is being asked to write this foreword for a wonderful, deserving person, and a good friend. Thank you, LeAnn. I am honored.

James E. "Obie" Evans

President

Dixie Softball, Inc.

A Word from the Book Collaborator

It's not often that a book collaborator gets to share their two cents about the authors they work with so when LeAnn asked me to share a few words I was humbled and thrilled at the idea. And, just so you know, as a writer, it's never *just a few words*.

The journey started earlier this year when I received a four-line email on February 11, 2019 from LeAnn which said, *Hi, my name is LeAnn Shelton. I'm from Pickens County, Alabama. The reason for writing is I'm looking for a "Sports Ghostwriter" to help with my autobiography. Do you know of anyone who would be interested in doing so? Thanks, LeAnn.*

She had done a Google search for sports ghostwriters, and thanks to my wonderful SEO expert, Fred Vinson of Lead Automation Systems, my website popped up near the top of the page.

The minute I read her email and viewed the links, I knew I had to bring this project to life! We scheduled a phone conversation and that was the clincher.

On the other end of the line I heard a kindhearted, caring woman whose heart pumped her desire to help humanity in any way she could.

My personal journey through helping LeAnn with her book has been wrought with both laughter and tears as I've worked through the chapters, one by one. Interviewing those closest to LeAnn—her mom, Deborah, her cousin, Dana, her former coach, Lee Gibson, and Heaven Harris's mother, Brittney—I came to appreciate the first-class, loving, kind people surrounding this courageous young woman.

I found myself envying (in a good way) the loving wisdom and positive attributes of LeAnn's mother and how she instilled in LeAnn a "can-do" attitude, something that eluded me with my own maternal parent. I thought *what a fortunate, blessed woman LeAnn is to be surrounded by these magnificent people who desire nothing more than to pour into each other's lives.*

Reading back through the transcripts I felt the pain and heartache of Brittney, Heaven's mother, as she recalled her daughter's accident and the internal struggle and healing she is still experiencing, yet I could *hear* the strength and resolve in her spirit. She and Deborah are cut from the same rugged cloth. As I re-read LeAnn's mom's words, a sense of profound admiration swept over me for this woman of strength. Tears would often well up as I relayed the sheer emotional and spiritual strength of this incredible woman. At other times, my laughter could not be muffled as I re-read stories about LeAnn's antics and how she put others at ease with what they *thought* was a disability. She showed them "disability" is only a word…a word she has never allowed to define her.

As I read Dana's words, I felt the heart of a caring, nurturing cousin who is ready and available to help in any way she can. And as I read Coach Gibson's words, I *saw* the wisdom and structure he imparted into these young girls' lives and the satisfaction he felt as he coached them from an undisciplined, ragtag team into a cohesive, well-oiled, winning team.

Personally, I have emerged from this project, this privilege, as a more grateful, humbler, and more insightful individual. I will always be thankful that LeAnn took a chance and reached out to me, and I know this is only the beginning of great things to come.

See, I told you it would be more than a few words, but some things cannot remain unsaid.

Michelle Hill

Your Legacy Builder at Winning Proof

Introduction
Play Ball!

This book didn't happen overnight. It wasn't just a thought I had one day that popped into my brain, *Hey, I think I'll write a book about my experiences*. This book started the day I was born. Its pages are marked by the love of my family and friends, worn around the edges with personal tragedy and loss, streaked with tears of defeat, and held together with the glue of unflinching faith and an unquenchable spirit of personal triumph.

It was clear at the beginning of this journey that I could not just write about the "what's" of all that has happened to me. There had to be more. The pages had to contain the heart and soul of who I am as a human being, as a softball player, as a daughter, sister, mother, wife, and friend.

Somewhere along the path of life, each of us will face moments of pain and loss in some shape or form. I simply never chose to allow loss to hinder me from all God had for my life and continues to reveal on a daily basis. Understanding *who* we are allows us to know *why* we are, thus giving our life purpose and joy.

If we were given a glimpse of all the circumstances of our life when we were young, a "coming-previews" sort of movie, what situations would we edit out? What circumstances would be included in the "deleted scenes?" *All* the bad? All the embarrassing? All the hurtful? All the loss? All the hiccups of life? How then would we expect to grow and mature and bolster our strength muscles? How would we develop any character or tenacity or determination?

The character Phil Connors (played by Bill Murray) in the movie *Groundhog Day* learned a valuable lesson in the mundane, the repetitive, the underbelly of life. After feeling like a victim of his circumstances, he finally realized that *he* was the one who could choose to change the reality of his daily life. Phil learns to love and he also evolves into being vulnerable enough to be loved. He gets there by first making a bunch of ridiculous mistakes. Phil then realizes that perfection won't save him either. Vulnerability and compassion are his ticket to a full life, bumps and all.

The truth is: none of us knows what any chapter of our story will uncover, or what characters will show up, or what the next scene will reveal. When we're born we can't predict what our childhood or adulthood will look like. Luckily, we don't know because we actually possess something so much more powerful; faith to know everything will work out exactly how it's supposed to. When you have the mindset of faith, everyone and everything around you helps guide you to reaching your goals and full potential. One arm was all I needed to fulfill my life's purpose and become an inspiration to so many more people than I would have ever imagined. The trick of life is to embrace all that is given us, the good and the bad, and use it for God's glory.

My hope and prayer is that as you read this book you will be filled with hope for your own set of circumstances. That every loss will be made whole within you. That you will understand there is purpose in your suffering whether you see it now or not. No matter what your situation, take the word "can't" out of your vocabulary. I hope my story shows you how!

1st Inning
Family Ties

"The memories we make with our family is everything."

Candace Cameron Bure

There's nothing like family. They come in all shapes, sizes, personalities, and quirks. Mine is no different. From my grandparents to my parents to my brother, I love my family, and each member's uniqueness is woven into the colorful fabric of my life, like a beautiful tapestry, vibrant with distinctive details and a few loose threads on the backside. Each member of my family has impacted and influenced my life in one way or another and I'm so very thankful for the heritage I received, and that my husband

and I are now able to pass down those timeless treasures of strong values to our son. Although this story is about *my* life, it would not be complete without introducing those who have played such an integral part in my journey. The following are my *cast of characters* who have helped shape my worldview in one way or another.

Grandmother Sanders

Grandmother Sanders, my grandmother on my dad's side, could always be found creating some special item from the vast amount of materials she kept on hand. Any kind of craft you could imagine. Woodworking too. Grandmother Sanders was a member of homemaker clubs, and also a teacher and librarian. She was always sewing, quilting, or cooking something special. People tell me I take after her with my creative side—I carved a cedar mantel above our fireplace in our living room and that is something Grandmother Sanders would have done.

Grandfather Sanders

I don't remember much about my grandfather Sanders except that he developed dementia. He lived in a home for people with dementia called Bryce Hospital and the only thing I recall is going to Tuscaloosa to visit him. The staff would wheel him into a white-walled, sterile waiting room and Grandmother Sanders would feed him ice cream and cake. Mom and Dad always told me he was a good man, and I believe it. I know he was a farmer; he owned a lot of farmland where he grew cotton, soybeans and corn, and he also raised cattle. Although I never really knew him, he is part of my heritage and I'm thankful for that.

Uncle David

Before my accident when I was two years old, my mother's brother, Uncle David, was swimming in a creek near our home. One day he dove in, hit a shallow spot, and broke his neck. He had to stay in the hospital and rehab for a long time but once he began to recover, my Grandma Guy brought him home from the hospital and took care of him. During that same time, she was keeping me while Mom and Dad worked. When Uncle David needed something to drink or eat, I was there to assist him. Even when he wanted a cigarette I would light and hold his cigarette while he smoked it. Luckily I never picked up his habit and to this day I hate cigarettes and cigarette smoke. Little did I know that just two years later I would be the one needing help doing basic tasks.

Looking back, I think by helping Uncle David God was preparing me for my challenges. Uncle David was a determined person. He had to learn how to walk, feed and dress himself all over again and I recall him telling me, "I can't wait to get back behind the wheel of my 18-wheeler!" I didn't think it was possible but you know what? Two years later he did just that. He set an incredibly positive example for me to follow.

My Dad, Woody

I had a loving, solid relationship with my dad growing up and that caring connection has continued through my adult years. I know he worked hard for our family and that gave me a sense of security and pride. Dad was a loving, caring man, the rock of our family. We never doubted his unconditional love for us, and his quiet demeanor did not equate to weakness of any kind. He led his young family with strength and resilience.

My Brother, Bobby

My brother Bobby with his big eyes and blonde hair is six years older than me. When we were children, he was my hero, especially when my accident happened. There are certain things about how he acts now that I don't particularly like, but I chalk that up to normal sister and brother stuff. I was always a tomboy so whatever Bobby was doing I was doing right alongside him. My mom recalls, "If you would give her a ball, a bat, or a bicycle, she was fine. Dolls? No way."

String, the three-legged dog

The summer after my accident, Daddy and Mom took us to buy a collie puppy. I never will forget that they let Bobby and me go into the pen to play and to each pick out our own puppy.

As I stepped into the pen I immediately eyed a dog with only three legs. The pen owners told us he was born that way. After my brother picked out his dog (he had to buy his), the owners gave me the three-legged dog that we named String and my dad made an artificial leg for him though I can't recall if String was really "into" that leg. I don't remember a whole bunch about String but one thing I do remember: String was there during the time after my accident and he became somewhat of a therapy dog for me.

My Mom, Deborah

I saved the best for last, not because my dad, Bobby, or my other family members are not important, or that I don't love them just as much, but because I have the closest relationship with my mom.

My mom is my rock. She's the epitome of a strong, fearless woman, and she's living proof that anything is possible. Mom is a motivator—she's one of those people who seems to have five extra arms; she can manage to hold onto a baby, two bags of groceries, and talk on the phone all at the same time. She has stood by me through my darkest times and loved me to the ends of the earth; not out of pity but out of a deep belief that anything is possible.

In 2013 I wrote the following letter to my mom and I'd like to share it with you.

Letter to My Mother

A mother daughter relationship is the most healing relationship in a woman's life. Yes, it has potential, it's a fact.

Because I'm bound to prove it.

Thank you for giving me life.

It's a gift we take for granted at times. Thank you for your belief in divine love healings to solve my physical limitations.

Thank you for my long toes to be grounded like you, and the taproot to Mother Earth.

Thank you for signing me up for softball to find my faith…not only in myself, but in life, to accept the things I can't change.

Thank you for laughing as loud as you want, no matter where you are. That laugh used to mortify me when I was around my friends. But now when I hear that same enthusiastic laugh come out of my own mouth, my friends tell me I sound just like you.

I'm so grateful you never quieted down.

Thank you for always telling me I could call no matter where I was or what I was doing, especially during my high school years.

Thank you for the ride home that one night I had too much to drink my senior year. And the next morning never asking any questions.

Thank you for accepting that I'm not perfect.

Thank you for being wacky and wonderful, always.

Thank you for being the mother my friends wished they had. Thank you for sticking up for me.

Thank you for the very big shoes you've given me to fill.

Some days I think it would be easier if I didn't have such a lofty legacy.

I would be comfortable with mediocrity; life would be easier in certain ways but so boring in others.

Thank you for setting the bar high even through my challenges in life. I give you the utmost respect for that. I've seen you give up your job to provide care for me. You have been and continue to be the most perfect mother for me.

Thank you for being all of you and letting me be all of me.

Thank you for playing all seven innings in my life, and sometimes overtime just by being my mother.

When I was growing up, my family lived out in the country. Pine trees, hardwood trees, lots of farmland, cornfields, hay fields, and our only neighbors were family members. Other neighborhood kids were cousins. We would spend hours swinging on the tire swing that my dad hung from a pecan tree in our backyard. My mom says I was "rambunctious, very active, sort of like a tomboy. We would take LeAnn and get her hair cut and the next day she would make me take her back to the beautician to have her hair cut shorter. She loved blue jeans and black shirts."

Each morning the McShan Lumber Company whistle blew and billowed its smoke at 7:00 a.m. and then again at 5:00 p.m. To this day that whistle blows at 7 a.m. sharp—it's the town's rallying cry that the day has begun and it's time to get to work. My husband and I recently moved closer to the sawmill so that whistle remains a staple of our daily lives.

When I was two years old my dad was in the trucking business and doing very well. But then hard times hit. The lumber mill my father hauled for burned down and as a result of Dad losing his job, we ultimately lost our home. It was really hard but as always, we adjusted to our "new normal" and kept on moving forward. My mom and dad rented an old house on my aunt's property; Aunt Annie Cockrell. Her grandkids, Dana, Stacy, and I had a ton of fun playing together on the land, whatever we could find to do; running, hide and seek, jumping rope, you name it.

My mom and dad worked very hard to save enough money to buy a used trailer. Finally, we had our own place again, but after we moved in and I turned three years old, I developed intestinal polyps. During the next nine months those polyps would have to be removed, and even at that young age, I recall having to swallow a lot of bad-tasting medicine in order to have the polyps removed. Swallowing that medicine was the worst part of my day back then.

My dad had started driving for a company called Butler & Company in Vernon, Alabama.

We didn't have but one car, an old Ford LTD. So, Mom would have to take Dad to work on Sunday nights. She would plop my brother and me in the back seat and we would sleep on the way there and on the way back, and when we got back home Mom carried us, one at a time, to bed. Then the next morning she got up early to take me to my grandmother Guy's house and to send Bobby off to school, and then head to work. Dad, at times, would stay on the truck for a week. On Friday nights Mom made the return trip with us kids to go pick up Dad and bring him home once again. This weekly routine went on for several months.

It was 1986 and school was out for the summer. This meant that Bobby and I got to stay at my mom's parents', Mawmaw and Pawpaw Guy's house. Bobby had started playing baseball so Pawpaw Guy drove Bobby and me to my paternal grandmother Sanders house so she could take Bobby and our cousin Jason to baseball practice. Jennifer and I played at the park while the boys practiced. We had fun climbing the jungle gym and running around in the grass. But all that was about to change…forever.

2nd Inning

The Lawnmower

"And we know that God causes all things to work together for good to those who love Him and to those who are called according to His purpose."

Romans 8:28

Grandmother Sanders lived in a brick house surrounded by farming land, and she had rock gardens for landscaping, and rocking chairs on the front porches. She kept the house as clean as a whistle and as neat as a pin. She was always cooking and the aromas coming from her kitchen always made us breathe in deeply to see what she had cooked up because we knew it was going to be goooood!

June 19, 1986 started out as a normal day for me and Bobby. My cousin Jennifer, Bobby, and I were playing in Grandmother Sanders' yard because Grandmother Sanders had told my mom that she missed us and wanted us to come play at her house. At that time, I was four and Bobby was ten. Jennifer had gone inside to call her mom, and Jason, her brother, was on one of those riding lawnmowers, cutting the grass. He was at the bottom of the hill, mowing, and then he headed up the hill to the house. Bobby and I continued to run and play around the house. As I ran around the house, my cousin Jason had already started up the hill with the motor in high gear. Bobby hollered at Jason to stop because he knew I was running around the back of the house.

Too late.

Before either of us knew it, my right foot was caught under the mower, almost cutting off my right little toe. As I tripped, I held up my left arm to protect my head and that's when the lawnmower splintered up my left arm at the elbow like a wood splitter. The lawnmower finally stalled but not until the blade severed my arm up to my left shoulder blade bone.

Bobby was both my hero and my angel. He darted toward me in an instant and with superhuman strength, his ten-year-old body lifted the lawnmower up off me and carefully unraveled my mangled left arm from the blade, then ran to get Grandmother Sanders. She bolted like lightning out to the yard and yelled, "Bobby, call your mother!" Bobby had picked me up and carried me into our grandmother's house. Blood was everywhere. I don't really recall what I was thinking at that time or how I was feeling as my body must have gone into shock.

Bobby called Grandpa Guy instead of our mom because he knew Grandpa Guy lived only half a mile away from Grandmother Sanders house. Through heavy pants he yelled, "Grandpa! Grandpa! Come quick, LeAnn had an accident and you need to take her to the hospital RIGHT NOW!" I'll always be thankful to Bobby for having the presence of mind to make that call instead of giving in to sheer panic.

Grandmother Sanders, meantime, had wrapped a towel tightly around my shoulder and arm. When Grandpa Guy came roaring up the driveway a minute later, they carefully but speedily put me in the front seat and rushed off to Pickens County Medical Center in Carrollton, Alabama.

I really don't remember much but I do remember Bobby leaning over from the back seat talking gently to me, "LeAnn, hang in there, we're almost there." I remember replying, "Bobby, I'm so sleepy." I had lost so much blood, but he kept telling me not to go to sleep. I don't remember much more than that because everything went blank.

The doctor on duty that day was Dr. Ben Crowder. He had been a doctor in the military during the Vietnam War and had treated a lot of trauma patients. He called my mother, told her who he was, and said, "I've got your daughter in the emergency room. There's been a mower accident and I need your permission to amputate her left arm."

How does a mother respond to something like that?

Deborah recalls asking, "Doctor, does she need to be flown somewhere else?" "No ma'am." He added, "She's not going to make it if she's flown anywhere, she's lost so much blood I'm going to have to do what I need to do." Deborah told him, "Do whatever you've got to do. I'll be there as soon as I can! And doctor, does she have any other cuts other than her arm?" "Yes, ma'am." And with that he hung up the phone.

My mom recalls what happened next. "I was working overtime as a supervisor at Kennedy Manufacturing Company, a garment plant, but after I talked with the doctor, and was visibly shaken, my friend and fellow employee Sandra Stripling drove me to the hospital in Carrollton, Alabama. When I got there LeAnn was already in surgery because the staff said they just couldn't wait. They had to give her a lot of blood to even get the surgery started. That's when I found out it was a lawnmower. And oh my, that was the longest night I believe I've ever spent in my life."

Dr. Crowder told her, "If we can make it through the night she's got a good chance but I can't promise you anything."

At one point the night nurse called for Dr. Crowder because they thought they had lost me.

When they finally took me to recovery, they let my mom come in and stay with me until they transported me to ICU. Mom describes the scene, "The first time I saw her when they let me go in, LeAnn's head was so swelled up they didn't even have time to brace her in order to get her sleeping medicine or the anesthesia just right, but her head had swelled up so badly that I barely recognized her. I stayed there with her all night in Intensive Care."

The fact that I had lost my arm didn't sink in until I woke up in ICU and asked, "Mom, where's my arm?" She didn't have an answer quite yet. How does a mother tell her four-year-old that she now has no left arm and has been plunged into a new reality that will last forever?

After I was in ICU for three days a nurse brought a rocking chair from the nursery for Mom to rock me. Mom recalls, "I picked LeAnn up so many times I got to where I could no longer pick her up over the rails, so I just sat and rocked her for hours and hours."

I also learned just recently when I crossed paths with one my nurses during that time, Rebecca Noland Richardson, that she had to bring her makeup bag to work every day because she would cry every time she came into my room.

I stayed in ICU for three days. Mom quit her job and devoted all her time to me, reassuring me, letting me know she would always be there. Talk about a mentally and emotionally draining time; we were all experiencing it at our own level. After all, I was trying to process it in my tender four-year-old mind, my brother in his ten-year-old mind, and my mom in her adult mind.

My mother later relayed to me that my cousin Jason's only concern was getting to baseball practice. He didn't seem upset at the fact that the lawnmower *he* was riding had taken my arm. Jason never came to see me or told me he was sorry or asked how I was doing. Apparently, even though the waiting room during my surgery was filled with church family and my mom's co-workers, I had simply inconvenienced Jason by delaying his getting to baseball practice.

On Saturday June 21st, they moved me to a regular room.

Before the accident, my father was headed to Oklahoma on a trucking haul, so he knew nothing about what had happened; my mom had just talked to him the night before and everything was just fine. They talked as usual and when they hung up I'm sure a looming disaster was the furthest thing from their minds. It was just another conversation.

After the accident Mom called Dad's dispatcher and told him what had happened, though she begged him not to tell Dad. "Just get him headed back to Alabama!" The company offered to fly him home once he checked in, but Mom told them no. We didn't have cell phones back then and making calls to anyone at any time wasn't possible so they told Mom it would be the next day before Dad reported in.

The next morning Mom called Dad's dispatcher to let him know I had made it through the night. All this time, my dad who had been driving the truck from Oklahoma toward Arkansas obviously had no idea what had happened. It was just another load he was transporting; anything other than the ordinary was not on his radar… until he talked to the dispatcher.

Dad headed home at the urgent request of his dispatcher, still not knowing his little girl was lying in a hospital bed with no left arm. I'm sure he experienced a few anxious moments not knowing why the dispatcher had urged him to hightail it home.

Mom knew Dad would be calling her on Friday night so she asked my Grandma Guy to spend the night at our house with my brother Bobby.

When Dad called, Grandma Guy told him Mom was sitting with a sick friend in the hospital and that she would be back home on Saturday morning.

Mom says, "I had never lied to Woody but I thought, *well this is something we must do in this circumstance for everyone's safety.*"

Saturday morning rolls around and Grandma Guy came and stayed with me at the hospital while Mom went home and waited for Dad's call. When Mom answered Dad's call, she could no longer hold back the tears; all her sorrow just flooded that phone line as she relayed the terrible news that the doctor had to amputate my left arm.

Mom says Dad just fell apart. She told him, "Look, you come straight on home and tell me what time you want me to pick you up." It was mind-boggling to Dad. A real shock.

I can't imagine what he was thinking during that unbearable five-hour drive from Arkansas to Vernon, Alabama. When he arrived home, Dad took two weeks off from work to help care for me and handle everything surrounding the accident. My mom quit her job. She says her only thought was *LeAnn needs me worse than we need the money, I just need to be with her.*

Toys, balloons, stuffed animals, and get-well cards filled my room—it looked like a toy warehouse had exploded and everything landed in my hospital room!

My cousin Dana recalls, "When it was time for me and my mom to go to the hospital for the first time after LeAnn's accident, we expected the worse, like her room would have a somber, serious atmosphere, but when we got there, LeAnn was sitting up in bed playing with all the stuffed animals. It wasn't anything like we imagined."

After six days in the hospital, on June 24 I got to come home. It took my dad two car loads to bring all the goodies home. My mom says I kept asking "Where's my arm?" because I was so bound down around my chest and shoulder. Mom told me, "Well, baby, you've been in an accident and the mower cut your arm and we had to patch it up with some stitches." At first I thought my arm was underneath all those bandages.

On Monday, June 30th, I had to go back to the hospital so the doctor could remove the two hundred plus stitches; they had to put me to sleep to take them all out.

After that, I couldn't stand to look at my shoulder and would constantly ask where my arm was. For two months after the accident, Mom says, I woke up several times a night, crying, yet I refused to talk about what happened.

My mom recalls, "When we took LeAnn home from the hospital, we took Bobby to my parents' house. Dr. Crowder had put him on medicine because he was so utterly traumatized by the whole ordeal. It was about three months after LeAnn's accident and Bobby was still not sleeping at night. In October of 1996, he was *still* not sleeping so we took him to a doctor in Columbus, Mississippi where he underwent a few therapy sessions and continued taking medicine so he could sleep. It was a really trying time for all of us."

Sometime after my accident my mom tried to get the homeowners policy information from Grandmother Sanders to help pay the medical bills since my dad's work insurance was not covering everything. My mom walked into Grandmother Sanders' house one day to ask about the policy number and Joe Sanders, Jason's father, was there. With a blatant attitude he told my mom, "Y'all got just what in the hell you deserved." My mom replied as calmly as she could, "I wouldn't wish losing a limb of a child on my worst enemy."

That was it. End of discussion. The Sanders side of the family seemed to go their separate ways after that; we only saw them at funerals or if we passed them going down the road. To this day we don't have much contact. Whenever Bobby and I went to Grandmother Sanders house after that day we noticed that she showed partiality between me, Bobby, Jason, and his sister Jennifer. They seemed to be the favored kids from then on.

Dr. Crowder had talked to me about getting a new arm but the pictures he showed me were the old-fashioned hook type of hand. I told him in no uncertain four-year-old terms that there was NO WAY I going to wear that! I thought it looked hideous and I refused to even consider it. I wanted an arm and hand that looked real.

Dr. Crowder sent me to Memphis, Tennessee for six to eight weeks of physical therapy and to see Dr. Tooms so I could be fitted with a prosthesis with fingers.

There was still a long road ahead, filled with adjustments for all of us, but what else *could* we do except adjust? This was our new reality.

3rd Inning

Adapting to Life with No Arm

On December 1, 1986, after three trips to Memphis, Tennessee, I got an early Christmas present; my first prosthetic arm. I had told the doctor that I wanted a hand that looked real. My whole family was there to cheer for me and my new arm. I was doing my best to use my arm efficiently and my mom was always there to help me learn new, better ways to use it.

My family was also hoping that my new artificial arm would ultimately be replaced with a battery-operated one but over time I found the extra arm cumbersome. It was heavy, and since I really couldn't do much with it, and it always seemed to be in my way, I eventually ditched it altogether. Even in elementary school, I'd come home with my arm in my bookbag.

My parents watched as I seemed to automatically use my knees or feet or mouth to accomplish daily tasks. They helped me when I really needed it but most of the time they let me figure things out for myself, and for that I'm grateful.

Mom says, "The adjustment of seeing our daughter having to learn how to do everything with one arm was much harder on my husband and me than on LeAnn. She was just so active as a child and really has never slowed down from her third day in the hospital and she's *still* going strong today in her role as a wife and mother and all the other activities she's involved in."

No one was surprised during the initial phase after my accident when I was the same old LeAnn when it came to neighborhood games. It finally came time to start my school years. On the first day of school my mom dressed me up in a real pretty purple dress, and she was just so proud of me and my purple dress. I came home and said, "Mama, I won't ever wear a dress back to school!" Mom says the only time she saw me wear a dress to school was when I was homecoming maid in high school.

When me and the neighborhood kids were young we played Hide and Seek and Red Rover, and then when I hit third grade we played reading games in the classroom. In fourth grade, 7up was the popular game. When fifth grade hit, outside games again became the norm; kickball, dodgeball, and softball. Sixth grade came and inside games made a comeback; checkers, chess, Monopoly, and UNO.

I'm thankful my family never showed me preferential treatment because I had one arm; I would not have wanted it anyway. In my mind, I was no different than anyone else. I was still a kid and I still had a lot of life to live. My mom used to tell people laughingly, "LeAnn doesn't get special treatment just because she has no arm, but she is spoiled. She's a typical tomboy who is active and always full of energy."

Once I got my stitches removed and was settled back at home, my parents bought a small pool for therapy which really helped me become more functional. Bobby would help me every day in the pool and with throwing and catching and balance.

My mom says, "I told God the night LeAnn laid there in that bed that even though she didn't have an arm,

I would do everything in my power to help her have a good life. I prayed for her to make it and I told God *we'll do the best we can with what we got*. So that's the way our attitude has always been; we don't live from a point of pity; we live from gratefulness.

"I quickly figured out there wasn't a whole lot I needed to do other than be a support to her. After her stitches were removed and she finished rehab we got her a bicycle. She was now five and her brother taught her how to balance and ride. One day he let go of the back of the bike and she didn't know he had let go and she just took off."

My mom remembers that she and Bobby tried to show me how to tie my shoes and the next thing they knew I was bent over with the string in my mouth and my feet up in Mom's lap, tying my shoes. Mom thought I'd always have to use Velcro-type shoes. Nope. I could tie my shoe strings as fast as any of them could.

Mom adds, "We're from the South and we all have gardens. We would be shelling peas or shucking corn, and LeAnn always found a way to do both. She'd put an ear of corn between her knees and shuck that corn just about as fast as I could. She loved to shell peas and snap beans too. I thought *Lord, there's nothing that child can't do!*"

There were a few difficult mental adjustments I had to overcome. For a long time, if anyone mentioned the word lawnmower, I would scream. I didn't want to talk about the accident at all!

Mom recalls, "When we would dress LeAnn she would hide the pad that covered her chest and shoulder; she would put her face against my breast and say, 'Mama, I don't want to see it, I don't want to see it!' It was a long time before she could look in the mirror. I kept telling her, 'Baby, life brings a lot of things, and although we don't understand it now, this is one of those things that we couldn't help and we're going to make the best of it.'"

Mom always told me the good Lord would never burden me with more than I could handle. Though sometimes it may have seemed like too much, I believed her words then, and I still believe them. Like everyone else I had good days and bad days and frustrating days.

Mom relays, "LeAnn, Bobby, and I, we all went to therapy. We had to have it. I would cry about it but I never let LeAnn see it. Sometimes you just have to talk things out with someone." Woody was on the road so he wasn't able to attend any therapy sessions.

The disappointments, tragedies, broken hearts, and loss of loved ones make us stronger. We tend to want to ask God *why* things happen to us, but I believe God doesn't do things *to* us, but rather *for* us. I believe God has a plan for everyone and there's a reason why everything happens. Though we may never know the reason, we must accept our circumstances through God's eyes.

Deuteronomy 29:29 in the Amplified Bible says, "The secret things belong to the Lord our God, but the things which are revealed and disclosed belong to us and to our children forever, so that we may do all of the words of this law." Some things we're just not meant to know; we simply submit to His plan.

His plan for each of us is like a fingerprint; no one has the same plan, and although circumstances may be somewhat similar, His reasons are different for each person. Whether it's losing a limb, losing your eyesight, getting cancer, battling through drug addiction, or losing a loved one, there's a reason and although we may not understand the reason we must have faith to know it will work out for good.

4th Inning

"Mom, I Wanna Play Softball!"

I marched into the kitchen one day at five years old and boldly proclaimed to my mom, "I wanna play softball!" Mom didn't skip a beat helping me find a team.

The thing was, the county we lived in didn't have enough girls for a girls softball team, so my very first season I had to play on the boys baseball team.

Boys can often be harsh to a girl playing on their team, but by the end of the season I was one of the guys and they actually looked forward to playing with me and wanted me to teach them how I learned the one-handed catch and throw. They accepted me onto the team and supported the way I had taught myself to maneuver my glove to catch and throw balls.

When I first decided at such a young age that I wanted to play baseball, catching and throwing posed a slight problem at the beginning but I was determined even then to overcome the obstacle. Bobby practiced with me for hours upon hours in our backyard while I developed a method of transferring the ball from my glove to my bare hand until I was as quick or quicker than a two-handed player.

What I did was catch the ball in my glove, flip the ball into the air, fling my glove to the ground and grab the ball out of the air to make the throw.

This method was hard to learn at first but with Bobby helping me practice, it soon become second nature and after a while I didn't even think about it. There were a few moments when I was first learning where I felt slightly frustrated but I just kept practicing every day.

Much later, Jan Swoope, writer for The Dispatch, said, "Softball gave Shelton challenges and hard knocks. But it also instilled in her discipline and dedication." I would say that aptly describes my journey.

I didn't see myself as being disabled in the least. Even at six, I wasn't focusing on my loss but rather I was thankful for what I did have…one good arm!

When my very first season ended and the boys team handed out awards, the grimace on my face and my audible sigh showed my displeasure at getting a trophy engraved with a picture of a girl in a ponytail on it. I was *not* that girly girl type.

The next year I tried out again but was cut from the team. I cried that whole summer, but luckily the next year we had enough girls for a softball team. I continued to hone my skills and improve as a player; I got faster, stronger, and learned the nuances of the game.

In 1993 when I was ten, I switched to Dixie Softball. In the Deep South, Dixie Youth Softball was and is the only kids' league that many people know. The league is based in Birmingham, Alabama and organizes hundreds of youth leagues in eleven Southern states, including Texas.

Dixie Softball can be quite nostalgic. Shortstops field grounders in dusty parks where their dads once played, and entire communities turn out for district tournaments leading to state competitions. The Dixie League afforded me great opportunities to develop as a softball player.

It was during that initial year playing in the Dixie League that I first heard of Jim Abbott, the one-armed pitcher who pitched for the Michigan Wolverines in college, the USA Olympic team, and two major league baseball teams. I closely followed Mr. Abbott's career—he was an inspiration to me, and a role model. Mr. Abbott heard later on about my softball success and sent me an autographed picture which to this day I cherish as one of my most prized possessions. I hope that someday I'll be able to meet Mr. Abbott face to face!

I played softball in the Dixie Softball League all through grade school and middle school and during that time my coaches came to respect my skill and determination because they could clearly see I was not a quitter nor one to give excuses of any kind. My coaches continued to treat me as any other member of the team and gave me no special consideration—I didn't want it anyway. All they saw was a young girl with an indomitable spirit and will to win.

In 1994, my second year playing in the Dixie League, Kevin Strickland, Pickens County Herald award-winning sports writer, wrote an article entitled *Where have all the heroes gone?* In the article he mentions several high-profile celebrities, noting bad behavior and pompous attitudes and flashy styles. Then he dials it down and tells readers where the real heroes are. He says, "Where have all the heroes gone? They're right here in our own backyards. They're on the football fields, on the baseball diamonds, and in the gyms around Pickens County. They're playing on Dixie Youth and high school teams— playing the games because they want to. They're pouring out their sweat and tears to play because the competitive fire burns in their hearts—not to play would be agony." I was honored when he mentioned me as a real live local hero.

In his article, Kevin continues, "You want a real hero? Look no further than Reform. That's where you'll find LeAnn Sanders. She was voted Most Valuable Player on her Dixie Youth softball team last season. She's a competitor and a classy young lady who played her heart out in every game. And she triumphed despite having only one arm. People like her are what the game of softball is truly about."

Because of Kevin's article I instantly became the spotlight of the town which in turn gave me the confidence to continue to play.

During my time on the Dixie Softball's Reform White Sox team, one of my coaches, Lewis Grace, had this to say: "If all the girls had [LeAnn's] determination and spunk, you'd have one great ball team."

The White Sox competed in a six-team league which included the Northside Rockets, the Northside Triple C's, the Riverside Skidders, the Myrtlewood Belles, and the Flatwood Looney Tunes. When I was 12 I was playing with the 13- to 15-year-old girls on the White Sox team. I had a special talent for obliterating baserunners in their tracks from my catcher's position, was named team MVP both years, batted over .500, I earned a spot on the All-Star team.

When it came time for the sub-district tournament, we lost to Cottondale 15-12, then we had a 12-2 loss to North Bibb, denying us the chance to advance to the district tournament.

Our coach, Larry Latham, said, "Pickens County All-Stars had the best team but simply didn't get the breaks they needed. We had the hardest, deepest hits of any team in the tournament but we just hit the ball right at people and couldn't get it to fall. That will get you beat every time."

We couldn't get the key hits we needed to control the game in spite of having the bases loaded two times during the game. We did however win the sportsmanship trophy for our team effort.

Coach said afterward, "We had a real good group of girls. They did everything I asked them to do, and they deserved to get the award. We all had a real good time together, and I think that's every bit as important as winning."

In July 1994, Kevin Strickland wrote an almost half-page article about me playing as a twelve-year-old with the older girls. I like his article because it not only focuses on my softball playing but on the other successes I've had in life. Successes like teaching myself how to shoot a rifle, running the Weed Eater, learning to play the trumpet in the band, and being an accomplished fisherman.

When I was six and first told my mom that I wanted to play baseball I announced, "I know there's a way I can do it if I can just get the chance." My mom agrees: "If LeAnn wants it, and puts her mind to it, there's nothing she can't do. Nothing is out of her reach."

I really had to remember what my mom said the year we were two games into the season. In 1995 I was batting a hearty .615 including a homer, two doubles, a triple and four singles. During the second game of the season I broke my leg sliding into home and was out the entire year. It was agonizing not to play but I knew I'd be out there as soon as humanly possible.

My mom tells people, "LeAnn has adopted a "can do" attitude about everything." She boasts as a proud mother, "LeAnn has managed to find a way to do just about anything. From the simple things like tying shoelaces, to shelling peas, or shucking corn; whatever we do, she can do it too."

I consider myself very fortunate and blessed to have a family who supports me, who has faith in me, and who have always encouraged me to believe in myself.

My mom echoes my thought with her own. "LeAnn has always been the type to try harder, to not give up. If she wants something, she really gets out there and works hard for it. The times she has told us she wants to do something we give her 100 percent support."

My cousin Dana (Dana's grandmother and my maternal grandfather were brother and sister) remembers the summer after the accident. "It was kind of amazing because our grandparents always grew big gardens and when they picked peas, LeAnn and I would sit on the couch and help shell them. She was shelling peas with her one hand better and faster than I could with two hands. Heck, she could even shell faster than any of the adults! From that time on LeAnn was determined to do whatever she needed to do to get along independently."

Dana continues, "When we were growing up, LeAnn and I were really more like sisters than cousins; we liked doing all kinds of things together. We rode four-wheelers and we loved to go to the river. We'd listen to music and just kill time; ride, talk, and have a good time. LeAnn is just a fun person to be around. It doesn't matter, wherever it is, she can make you laugh. She's really quiet when around a bunch of people, but get her around family, or a one-on-one and she's like a different person. She's wide open and hilarious."

In 1998, my freshman year at Pickens County High School, I stepped up as both starting fast-pitch pitcher

(4.20 ERA) and leading hitter (.500 average for the Lady Tornadoes topping all five Tornado pitchers) and I actually ended up starting all four years, an All-Star every year—I played outfield and had a high stolen base record.

My coach at the time, Kevin Strickland, described me as "extremely competitive and extremely aggressive." He said, "The fact that [LeAnn] is playing with a limitation never occurs to her." Under Coach Strickland's leadership, I pitched a no-hitter in one game which was quite a feat.

My coach after Kevin Strickland was Coach Lee Gibson, who at first we all thought was worse than a military drill sergeant. He was so hard on us; he had coached football so he treated us like football players—he pushed us so hard. I would come into my house after practice and cry because my body ached so bad from his drills.

The girls on our team were falling asleep during classes because we didn't get out of practice until we ran our laps and that was after seven o'clock in the evening. What time he ended practice depended on how fast we ran our laps. That year half the girls on the team almost quit because of his coaching style but we managed to hang in there that first year.

Coach Gibson has his own version. "I had no intentions of ever coaching a girls softball team; wasn't on my radar at all. I was a football coach and because of an incident that happened I was told at Christmas that at the first of the year I would be the new softball coach. I didn't know anything about coaching girls softball but we will do the best we can do. All the girls were freshmen and sophomores that year. I saw them through and I think I coached one more year of softball after that. After that, I gave up softball and just focused on football. But that was a special group of girls."

Coach says, "Yeah, the girls' team kind of got away with a lot before I got there. From what I gather they ran the ship before I took over but it didn't take long to figure out I meant business."

Coach's philosophy is, "I think every child, student-athlete, and people in general want to have discipline, they want to have a set structure and a way of doing things. The girls' team, in time, saw the great things they could achieve with some discipline and hard work, and that's what they did."

Amazingly, the second year wasn't as bad because Coach Gibson had our team in shape. He made us realize that we could be the best, we just had to work HARD for it. We became county champs and it was the first time in many years that the Lady Tornadoes had won big. He made us believe in ourselves and never give up. He showed us that it didn't matter how strong we were but that if we believed in ourselves, that would make us winners...and we were!

The four years Coach Gibson coached, all of us girls achieved a lot of our goals. We never thought we'd actually thank him for the hard, grueling workouts he made us do but in the end, we did, every one of us. After it was all said and done, we loved and adored Coach Gibson and after that first year we respected him.

I could write a book about just him and what he did for our team. Below is a letter I wrote to Coach Gibson expressing my thankfulness for his toughness and direction:

Dear Coach Gibson,

Having you as a coach helped me realize what I needed to do to be successful, not only in softball, but also in life. I will always be grateful for your valuable input and investment in my life. This letter is a reminder that your hard work and time didn't go unnoticed. I value everything you did to make me become the best athlete. You are truly the best coach ever. A coach like you comes only once in a lifetime. The Lady Tornadoes were blessed to have you—thank you for being our strength. The happiness and success you brought into our lives can't be measured.

Thank you for being the person you are!

Coach Gibson once said, "[LeAnn] is the type of softball player every coach dreams of having. She is a tremendous athlete. She's got a very strong, competitive spirit; she just loves the game and I could tell that from the first minute I watched her play. I don't have to worry about her. She's definitely a leader on the team, and she's so motivated. If any coach had nine of her, they wouldn't lose very many games."

I'm thankful Coach Gibson didn't see me as any different than any other player. There was never any doubt in my mind that whatever my teammates could do, I could do, and like anyone else on the team, I was out there to compete and win.

I played pitcher and outfield.

Coach Gibson remembers, "LeAnn's strengths were her tenacity, her love for the game, and the way she played and practiced. It was all business all the time. This is my twenty-second year in athletics and I would compare her drive and focus to anyone I've ever coached. But you know, having a disability of playing with one arm, LeAnn always thought she had to prove something, and she never saw herself as even having a disability. She could bat right-handed *and* left-handed. She pitched a lot for us until I decided for her safety that she didn't need to pitch anymore because she took a few off the leg and the chest. So for her safety, I decided it wasn't smart for her to continue to pitch. I think she got mad about that, but I put her out in the outfield.

"I remember her playing in one particular game, and you know it's hard enough to catch a ball with two hands and throw a runner out, but we were playing Tuscaloosa at the time. LeAnn was playing center field and they hit a ball; she caught it and the girl tried to tag a base and she threw her out—it was one of those moments that I will always remember.

"We had a cohesive team and we never let our typical teenage girl bickering get in the way of softball. We would sometimes get our nose out of joint when one girl started to date somebody's ex-boyfriend or something like that, but we never let it affect our practicing or playing and that made our group special. We cared about winning. We cared about competing. We won a lot of ball games and had a lot of fun. And I believe if you go and look at the school records for that three- or four-year period they won more softball games than they ever had or have since and that's a testament to those girls and their dedication to hard work and discipline."

One article by Steve Irvine in Tuscaloosa Magazine described my journey very accurately, "[LeAnn] wasn't a one-armed player clinging to softball. She was an outstanding player who just happened to have one arm." I was honored that first year to receive a Who's Who in Sports All Stars award for being one of the nation's outstanding athletes. All because I didn't quit!

It's so nice to know that my life has served to inspire others to reach their full potential. Local writer David Cooper wrote an article for the Tuscaloosa News Sports Section about not quitting and having endurance to finish what you start. On May 25, 1998, I received this wonderful letter in response from the Tuscaloosa Amateur Athletic Association. whose goal is to recognize amateur athletes for their accomplishments.

Ms. LeAnn Sanders
C/O Pickens County High School
Reform, AL 35481

Ms. Sanders,

[David Cooper's] recent write-up in the Tuscaloosa News Sports Section was inspirational, to say the least. So much so in fact that I, as a volunteer Fast Pitch Softball coach here in the Tuscaloosa area coaching young ladies 12 years old and under, plan on using this article as a lesson in "STICK-ABILITY!"

Gene Stallings, University of Alabama National Champion Football team coach, made this statement when asked at a press conference who his best players might be. "The player with the best natural ability to play football may not be the best player on the field. I've found that a player with outstanding desire, dedication, and discipline, who works hard—then comes back and works even harder is often the BEST player on any team. Every man on this team that meets this criteria is my best player."

Ms. Sanders, you are a "BEST PLAYER" in anyone's book of sports. Your parents, family, and coaches must feel the same way about you. I would conclude this note by saying "Good Luck" in the future but somehow I don't think luck plays any part in your future or your approach to the great game of Fast Pitch Softball.

Sincerely,

J.L. McCutchen, Pres.

Tuscaloosa Amateur Athletic Assn.

Letters like these make everything I've been through worth it, knowing that my legacy is far-reaching and impactful. Mr. McCutchen's letter simply proved that there's more to life than sports although I admit sports are pretty darned important.

My high school years weren't ALL sports. Between games and seasons I had a chance to be a normal teenager. My friends and I would listen to rap music, gulp down lots of Coca Cola, learn to drive, and we were old enough now to go out on the weekends. A major highlight was being elected as a Junior Maid for homecoming. The not-so-fun part was getting used to the braces on my teeth.

I never wasted an opportunity to joke with my friends. Like the time my driving test was cancelled due to rain. I told them, "I'm ready to do it and at least you know I won't drink and drive or eat anything while I'm at the wheel." I think my sense of humor put everyone at ease and as my mom always said, "It's better to laugh than cry." Another time I told some friends I was going to get my nails done at half price. They were like, "Really? Where?" It hadn't even occurred to them that I was joking and that's what made it so funny.

Coach Gibson knew I was like every other teenager. He tells people, "You know LeAnn had a silly side; she'd cut up off the field. But she took her schoolwork seriously, she took her relationships seriously. For LeAnn, being a friend meant something more than just *saying* you were friends. She was always there for everybody. I think she was a role model off the field with her behavior. She never got in trouble, never did anything to sacrifice what she was trying to do on the softball field. And those things make her who she is. When she sets her mind to doing something, her whole life revolves around making sure she accomplishes that goal."

Coach Gibson also remembers me telling him one time that the only thing I wished I could do was clap. Coach says, "I was kind of a smartass back in the day so my wife and I went to Mardi Gras and I just happened to see one of those toys that was a clapper and I brought it back to LeAnn. She loved it and said she would keep it forever. Also, her left arm is the one she lost so I would call her Lefty and she said I had big feet, that I looked like Mr. Ed. We engaged in that type of friendly, joking banter all the time."

During my high school years I must have listened to my favorite song, *It's a Great Day* by Travis Tritt, a million times. That song was just so uplifting and refreshed my soul every time I listened to the lyrics. I also relished time with my friends while we watched *Remember the Titans* and my favorite TV show, *Martin*. Of course when my friends and I reached our senior year a slew of fun activities encircled all of us like picking out a class ring, posing for our senior portraits, and ordering all of our caps and gowns for graduation, each of us knowing that a new form of freedom was right around the corner.

Although the Pickens County High School Lady Tornadoes were a force to be reckoned with, there were some losses along the way that kept us grounded and working harder for the next win. In one game the Carrollton Lady Indians outslugged us in a super close battle that ended with us losing, 21-20. To be that close and then to lose, well…suffice it to say…we didn't like losing.

Another time those pesky Carrollton Lady Indians got us again with an 11-1 win by racking up runs and pitching us out of the game. They had seven runs in the second inning alone and three runs in the third inning and that threw our game off and handed them the win on a silver platter. I pitched for one inning during that game, giving up four hits, two walks and two earned runs. The other pitcher and one of my best friends, Abby Woodard, completed four innings, surrendering three hits, seven runs, striking out three and walking six. That game just wasn't ours.

Then there was the year when we lost out on going to the state tournament. The Pickens High School Lady Tornadoes fell short when Hale County beat us in two games to shut us out of the state tournament for the third straight season. We had dominated the regular season under Coach Gibson and then we were forced to go on the road for a sub-state best-of-three against the Lady Wildcats.

During that time Coach Gibson told local reporters, "We played pretty well in the first game. We spotted them a couple of runs and then battled back into the game. We just didn't take advantage of some opportunities. it was a tough one to lose."

Game two of that three-game series, the Lady Tornadoes made error after error but then bounced back to even up the game, but then more errors gave the Lady Wildcats a 10-4 advantage to win. We all knew we hadn't played our best game and Coach Gibson felt really bad for us seniors; Abby Woodard, Jalynn Abrams, Kim Taylor, and I, because he really wanted us to end our final season with a win.

Of course, wins are always more fun! One April in 2000, we posted a 13-4—a school best—as we upped our season record to 16-12. We had a four-game sweep that season, downing the Aliceville Jackets and Greensboro Lady Raiders in double headers. Against Aliceville, we scored ten runs in the bottom of the first, three more in the second, two in the third and another run in the fourth inning. A final score of 16-8 felt awesome!

One incident stands out when I recall our games with Aliceville. In my junior year during a game I was on the mound throwing K's (strike-outs). We were ahead by several runs and their coach said a player should have a glove on while on the pitching mound and he tried to get me thrown out of the game. My mom hadn't made it to the game yet but my "family" of teammates, moms, dads, and grandparents took up the slack for me. Even the umpire wasn't happy! When you see an umpire take off his mask and point to a coach, it's never a good thing. Needless to say, I stayed on the mound.

We then traveled to Greensboro, Alabama to take on the Lady Raiders where we won 15-9 in the opener and 9-8 in the second game of the double header. I pitched three innings that game and surrendered no hits. Abby pitched two relief innings and kept us winning. There were a few moments where it was awfully close: in the fourth inning, the Lady Raiders closed to within one in the bottom of the inning and we narrowly escaped a bases-loaded one-out jam with a double play.

Pickens County comprises four cities (Reform, Gordo, Carrollton, Aliceville) and I'd have to say that Gordo was our primary rival within those four cities. They took every chance they got to prevail over us and take wins we thought we had.

Coach Gibson remembers it a little differently. "We used to beat the mess out of Gordo. Anytime we beat Gordo, that was good. We won some big games and some tournaments against the bigger teams. We made it to sub-state a couple of times."

Also in 2000, the Lady Tornadoes participated in the first annual American Christian tournament (ACA) in Tuscaloosa. The ACA tournament was held in a round-robin format with the top two teams advancing to a championship game.

Our team dropped an opening round decision to Holy Spirit, 12-9, even though we held the lead, 7-5, heading into the fifth inning…that was before Spirit rallied to plate with seven runs, giving them the victory. ACA prevailed against us 11-3 in a rain-soaked championship game.

In the second round of the ACA tournament we triumphed over American Christian 12-8 with Abby and I making strong pitching performances and Abby taking a feed from our catcher Kim Taylor that erased a runner attempting to steal home for the game's final out.

And then with a championship game berth on the line, we completely obliterated South Lamar 32-6 in the third game of the day to take the second place trophy. The championship game ended up being a re-match of our duel with ACA earlier in the day. Unfortunately, I didn't have a good game. I allowed ten runs on eight hits in three and a third innings. At least we took second place and I know we played our hearts out.

On March 1, 2000, when I was a junior, the Pickens County Herald reported in an article, "Junior centerfielder LeAnn Sanders is the key to the Lady Tornado outfield." They also cited Cindy Tunnell, Lindsey Keasler, Kim Taylor, Robyn Grace, and Lena Bass as being key players for the Lady Tornadoes. I'm so humbled and proud that during my high school years I received a Varsity Letter Award for all the seasons I played but the one I am most proud of is the Certificate of Achievement I received on May 5, 2000, for having the Highest A Average (11th in U.S. history). Now that took a lot of muscles and work…brain work that is.

Also in 2000 we hammered South Lamar Lady Stallions 14-4 with 22 hits, at least one run in each of the game's six innings. Our leadoff hitter, Jessica Hill, started our 22-hit barrage with three hits including a homer and two RBIs while Jalynn Abrams cleaned up with single, a triple, a home run and three RBIs. We each took our turns slamming hits to pummel the Lady Stallions. Nobody could stop us that game! Under Coach Gibson we had a tight, well-oiled team that loved to win together.

"I think just not acting or thinking like a victim has made LeAnn the person she is," says Coach Gibson, "and I think she's trying to pay that forward and show people it doesn't matter what your circumstances are, all you've got to do is put your left foot in front of your right foot and keep moving and the day will get better. Her example fully demonstrates that you can accomplish whatever you want to do."

Coach no longer coaches. He's a system-wide Athletic Director for our school system. He says, "I have a four-year-old now and the AD position gives me time to go home and spend time with my son. Last year (2018) was my last year of coaching and when my son gets a little older I will probably get back into it. But right now this is a good break for me." Coach hesitates. "Well I take that back, I *am* coaching, I'm coaching his tee-ball team."

Although his direction has shifted, Coach Gibson is always ready with a positive, uplifting word. He recently told an interviewer, "I'm proud of the woman LeAnn has become and I know she's a good mother so I wish her the best in whatever she decides to do in the next chapter of her life."

I must relate one strange story in the midst of my high school softball-playing days. I call it the night I challenged God. It was a late night in high school after softball practice. While lying in bed I found myself in a deep prayer to the point that tears started to roll down my face. The fact that it was a particularly hot night and our central air conditioning had gone out made the atmosphere heavy with heat even with the small air unit lodged in my bedroom window.

While I was praying, I challenged God. I said, "God, if you really hear my prayers, give me a sign."

I had a small white trash can on the side of my bed under the window. When I opened my eyes the white trash can was GLOWING. Yes GLOWING! So bright that it was lighting up my whole room. It seemed to thump as if it had a heartbeat.

I was so scared—I lay there frozen in my bed. I threw the covers over my head trying to figure out if I needed to run to my parents' room.

I determined that was a wise course of action so after working up the nerve, I started to run out but just as I made it to my bedroom door, I stopped and thought to myself *I've got to find out what it is that's making my trashcan glow.*

I inched quietly and carefully over to the trash can and discovered it was a lightning bug. Apparently it had flown in through the small window unit air conditioner.

At least I didn't need to run to my parents' room now that my mysterious visitor was identified.

Needless to say I never challenged God again!

I continued to play after high school, signing on with adult leagues. I played until I was 29 years old, a 24-year playing span for which I am proud. I continue to stay in touch with several of my teammates and especially Coach Gibson. As a matter of fact, I built a rocker for his son when I got into woodwork.

Coach shares: "That rocker remains in his room, and even now at four years old, he still sits in that rocker and reads his books; it's a very special item in our household."

Unexpected Honors

One day in 2013 I was inside the house busying myself with the day's chores when the phone rang. To my surprise it was Dixie Softball's President and Founder, James E. "Obie" Evans. What shocked me more was when he told me I was getting inducted into the Dixie Softball Hall of Fame Class of 2013. To say I was amazed and humbled is an understatement. When I hung up,

I remember that I couldn't stop smiling. I thought *what an incredible privilege*! I knew I had to share the accolade because anyone who plays any kind of sport knows that it takes more than just one person to accomplish anything on the field or court, or wherever. Overcoming adversity and flourishing requires a "village" of support. Here is the thank you I sent after they inducted me into the Hall of Fame:

> *I would like to thank the Dixie softball Hall of Fame Committee and Mr. Obie Evans, President of Dixie Softball Inc., for inducting me into the Dixie softball Hall of Fame Class of 2013. I am honored and humbled to be chosen for such an incredible privilege and I will always reflect on the moment with great pride. After I lost my left arm in a lawnmower accident at the age of four, Dixie Softball is where my love for the game of softball began. It had a big influence on my life and has shaped me into the person I am today. It provided a passion for the game and gave me the reason to overcome the obstacles in my life. Also, it taught me discipline and the meaning of hard work and dedication. In any sport you play, it takes more*

than just one person to achieve accomplishments like being inducted into the Hall of Fame. It takes a lot of encouragement, support, and love of family, friends, coaches, and teammates. So I decided to honor them all. That's what sports are all about; it helps create a strong foundation for what type of person you will become later in life. I will always cherish the memories during those years and I want to thank everyone who has supported me and guided me during such a memorable time in my life.

In 2015 the Dixie Softball National Board of Directors created the *LeAnn Sanders Shelton Dixie Softball, Inc. Courage Award* in my honor. I had no idea when they asked me to speak at the National Dixie Banquet in Nashville, Tennessee that they were going to reveal this award. They give it to players who show determination and courage, and honestly, I was humbled once again that they would create an award in my name.

During my speech I spoke what was in my heart. "Dixie Softball gave me the determination to overcome the impossible. My softball success is impacted due to the mentorship from Dixie Softball. It will forever remain a major contribution behind my achievements in life. To Dixie Softball, thank you for the 88 red stitches that truly held my life together."

Obie Evans said, "LeAnn epitomized who Dixie Softball wanted to honor with its courage award." He continued, "When we decided to present the Dixie Softball Courage Award, we wanted to present the award to LeAnn Sanders Shelton because of her great courage to overcome the loss of an arm as a small child and become an all-star player where she led her team in hitting, stealing bases and as a dominant pitcher and outfielder. Not only was it her playing ability years ago but Dixie Softball appreciated the moral person that LeAnn had become and the fact that the loss of her arm did not stop her from charging into life with the tenacity that she possessed when she played Dixie Softball."

People have asked me what softball has meant in my life. I always respond, "Oh, I love it. I don't think I'd be me without softball," although I will add an important point: my life as a whole consists of much more than softball; it's all about faith, family, and friends.

Red Stitches Photographs

First Christmas 9 months old 12/25/1982

LeAnn 2 years old and Brother Bobby 7 years old Christmas

Family Portraits: Mom, Dad, Brother Bobby

Christmas Tree 4 years old 12/25/1987

Red Stitches

Christmas Tree 4 years old 12/25/1987

Five Years Old with Brother Bobby age 10 years old

6 years old First time playing baseball City Park in Reform AL 1993

Junior Year of High School Won Jr Maid homecoming

LeAnn and Jalynn Abrams Gray Won award Captain's award teammate

Softball Senior Portrait 2001 with trophies

School Picture 2000 Pickens County Lady Tornado Softball Team

Graduation 2001 with Kim Taylor and Jamie Moore from Pickens County High School

LeAnn and Jeremy Skidder Wedding day with Big Barrels

LeAnn and Jeremy Skidder Wedding day with Big Barrels

LeAnn and Jeremy Wedding 8/19/2006 Union Hill Church

LeAnn and Jeremy Wedding 8/19/2006 Union Hill Church

LeAnn and Jeremy Wedding 8/19/2006 Union Hill Church

LeAnn and Jeremy Wedding 8/19/2006 Union Hill Church

Wedding Day Mom and Dad

LeAnn and Cousin Dana Moorhead Wedding Day

LeAnn and Jeremy Fall Picture 2 years of Marriage 2008

LeAnn and Jeremy 2009

Columbus Ms Prospt Park 2011 Playing for Church League Columbus Christain Center

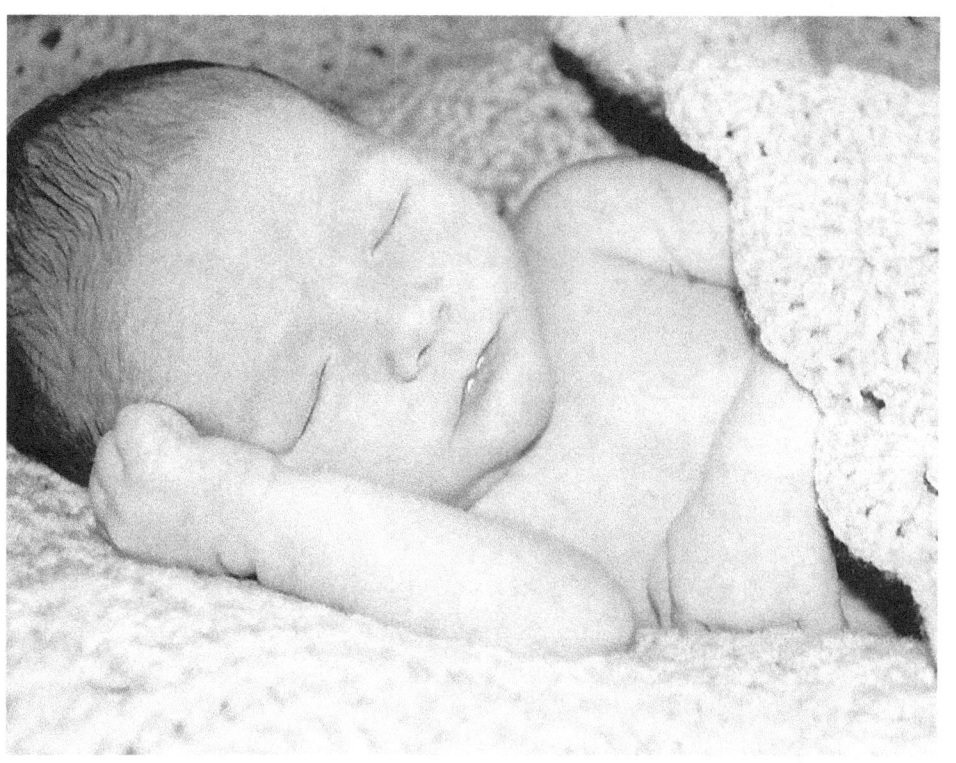

Gunner Lake Shelton 4 days old 8/31/2012

Gunner Lake at one and half years old

LeAnn and Gunner Lake 2014

Gunner Lake Shelton Family Reunion Easter 2014 Gordo Alabama

LeAnn and Gunner Lake at home Christmas after school play 2016

LeAnn and Heaven First time meeting in Sylacauga Alabama

LeAnn and Heaven walking after surgery at UAB Hosipital in Birmingham Alabama

5th Inning

Jeremy and Gunner Lake

It was 2004 when my cousin, Dana Moorhead, and my friend, Vicky Brown, decided to play matchmaker. Jeremy was working for Brown Logging and Vicky's husband was one of the owners of the company. All of them were into racoon hunting so Vicky invited me to one of the coon hunts to meet Jeremy.

Dana recalls, "LeAnn had not been out with anybody for a while, and Jeremy worked for the logging company that my best friend Vicky's family owned. Vicky and I started thinking out loud about Jeremy and LeAnn and I was like, "Hey let's see what happens with this!"

We knew LeAnn had always liked hunting and fishing so we thought they would make a good couple. They ended up going out and there it was; history in the making."

Jeremy had no idea I was there specifically to meet him and after our initial meeting it took him two weeks to call me, although he said he knew right away he was going to marry me—at the time though, he couldn't believe I wanted to meet him.

Jeremy relates, "About three or four years before LeAnn and I met, me and Roger Brown (one of the owners of the logging company I was working for) were in town at a Car Quest parts store. When we were getting out of the work truck to go into the store, LeAnn pulled up at the gas station across the street. Roger nudged me and said, "Right over there is a good little lady." I laughed and told him, "She would never give a guy like me a chance." I honestly thought LeAnn was too good for me. I thought to myself, *I'd never have a chance with that woman.* What I didn't know at the time was that she was praying for me. To my surprise, four years later I would marry that stuck up girl."

When Jeremy finally did call and we had a chance to talk, I knew he was the one I would marry. I had prayed for a man like Jeremy—he was in fact everything I had prayed for which was someone to love me with graceful eyes, to see me through my flaws, a best friend to make me laugh and a shoulder to cry on. And for some odd reason I knew he was going to be left-handed; call it woman's intuition, but I just knew. I trusted God that He would bring everything I needed in His timing. And I knew God had Jeremy saved especially for me, just like He faithfully saved me for Jeremy.

Jeremy proves to me daily that my prayer was answered. I thought I couldn't fall harder in love than when he and I first met but here I am married 13 years and I am deeper in love than I've ever been. True love really does exist and so do God's promises. God knew the simplest desire of my heart down to the intricate details and stored up an abundance of blessings for me just from simply asking and committing myself to His will. God is concerned about every area of your life, especially the person you will marry. He desires to give you good things but they have to be in His time. But back to dating…

I'm a huge steak lover so during one of our dates, I ordered a steak and Jeremy automatically cut it for me. There was no question in his mind what he should do; he did it so naturally with such a caring spirit.

On another date we went to a Hibachi grill, a Japanese style restaurant where random people sit around a large grill and the chefs cook up the dinner, usually with some humor thrown in. Well, during dinner this particular night, the chef was singing happy birthday in Japanese to someone at our grill and had urged everyone at the table to clap during the song. When he was about half way through the song, he looked at me and said, "You not clap." I think he was thoroughly embarrassed when he figured out the deal.

Jeremy and I dated 11 months before he asked me to marry him—we had talked about getting married over the course of the year and had even looked at rings. He proposed to me after taking me out to eat one night. We had had dinner at our favorite sushi restaurant and went Christmas shopping afterward before heading over to my parents' house where we unloaded all the gifts we had bought. Jeremy was getting ready to leave to get back home when suddenly he stopped, dropped down on bended knee and asked me to marry him.

There was no question that I would say anything but yes...and I did!

Our wedding day was August 19, 2006 and I can honestly say that it was one of the best days of my life! Weather was beautiful...hot...but beautiful. We got married at Union Hill Church; nothing fancy, nothing expensive. It wasn't about that anyway. We loved each other and wanted to spend our lives together and that's all that mattered. I wore a dress given to me by Dana, the same cousin I grew up with and whose matchmaking efforts had proved successful. Jeremy's cousin, David, married us. After the ceremony we left the church in a skidder[1] with big barrels that had a "Just Married" sign attached to the back. For us, it seemed like a logical means of post-wedding transportation since Jeremy worked in logging.

Unlike most newly married couples who may have major adjustments to make after they say "I do," we had an excellent first year; during that year Jeremy got a new job at BF Goodrich in Tuscaloosa, Alabama with better pay and benefits so that was really the only major change we experienced and we are thankful we didn't have any other major life changes during our initial year.

---

[1] A skidder is a heavy vehicle used in a logging operation for pulling cut trees out of a forest.

Jeremy continues to this day to support me in anything I set out to conquer, including deer hunting and fishing. I adore bass fishing so I made a leather belt adapted for deep sea fishing with added suspenders, a pipe fitting to hold my pole, and an array of small tools. Throughout our marriage and my life I've tried various prosthetic limbs but I always end up abandoning them because I find them heavy and clunky but all that doesn't even matter to Jeremy. He loves every part of me. In fact, he tells people, "Yeah, LeAnn's got another arm but it just sits on the end of the bed."

We have continued a happily married life with no significant issues. And that's not to say we don't scrap every once in a while but for the most part we get along very nicely and we do our best to put each other's needs before our own.

At first I didn't want kids. Then I started seeing my friends having babies and I changed my mind. In my heart I knew that if Jeremy and I ever did have a child, it would be a boy…but two years went by and no baby. Sometime during November 2011 I told Jeremy that if we didn't get pregnant after I turned 30 we would stop trying because I just didn't see myself pregnant after turning 30. Ironically, I was actually pregnant at the time I said those words although we didn't find out until the next month.

In December 2011, Jeremy and I went on a hunting trip. When we arrived at our destination, he dropped me off near a deer stand[2]. I had to walk down a short road to get to it and when I got there I started to feel sick. I didn't think much of it and was sure the feeling would pass after I sat down for a moment. It didn't. There wasn't good phone service in the area—we used two-way radios so I paged Jeremy to tell him I wasn't feeling well and he headed back to pick me up. On the way home I was thinking *why am I feeling so sick all of a sudden?* It didn't click until we got back into town and then a giant bright light bulb lit up in my brain. I said, "Jeremy, we need to stop and get a pregnancy test." He gasped, "Whaaat?" The result? Two little pink lines. We were pregnant!

---

[2] A deer stand can be either an open or an enclosed platform used by hunters. The platforms are secured to trees in order to elevate the hunter and give him or her a better vantage point.

Man, that nine months went by fast! The morning of August 27, 2012 after getting out of bed, my water broke. I woke Jeremy up. I called my mom and she told me to get in the shower. After getting out of the shower I started to have sharp pains and that's when Jeremy called my mom back in a frantic frenzied tone. "Ms. Deborah, she's ready!" Mom told him to go take a shower too and she would leave right away for our house. By the time she got there Jeremy was freaking out—he told my mom that we had to leave ASAP because he was sure I was going to have the baby on the side of the road.

Gunner Lake came into the world on August 27, 2012 at 11:45 p.m. at Druid City Hospital in Northport, Alabama in the Women's Pavilion, weighing in at seven pounds two ounces and a height of 19 and a quarter inches. We named him after two of our favorite hobbies: hunting and fishing.

I believe Gunner Lake and I had the best nurses in the world tending to us. My nurse was Holly Lowery and the doctor who ushered him into the world was Dr. Joanne Myers. Holly was an outstanding nurse and was also from the same town I grew up in so we got along excellently.

After Gunner Lake came into our world our lives revolved around him, and still do. He seemed to sense the things that were hard for me to do like picking him up and changing his diaper. When he was six months old I could tap him on his shoulder and say, "Pick-up." He would get up on all fours so I could get my arm around him to pick him up.

Dana had always told me, "I'm going to wait and see if you can handle a kid before I have one. She was my guinea pig for motherhood. If she could, then I would give it a try."

Dana adds, "LeAnn did a wonderful job with Gunner Lake. When I had my little girl, Preslee, I probably called her a thousand times asking questions about what to do. I know I can count on LeAnn for anything I need and she knows that whatever I can do to help her with anything at home or Gunner Lake, we're always there for each other. And it's a good feeling to know that you have somebody like that in your corner."

The toughest part of motherhood with one arm was definitely changing diapers but Gunner Lake learned to pick his little bottom up for me to put the diaper under him. I always had to change him sitting on the floor because I had to use my feet to change him. Jeremy was great about picking up the slack and really, he often still leaves me speechless when I observe what a great father he is to Gunner Lake and he's certainly the best husband a girl could ever have.

After we moved into our new house Jeremy was still working the swing shift at BF Goodrich so some nights it was just me and Gunner Lake. When it was time for bed we would head upstairs and of course that meant I had to carry him. Once we got upstairs I had to flip on the lights with him in my arm. One day out of the blue Gunner Lake reached out and flipped on the light switch. At first I didn't realize what he was doing. I never had to do it myself again because it was like a norm for him from then on.

I didn't want much help and I rarely asked. "She never asked for help," Dana remembers. "That's just how LeAnn is, and it was amazing because there were little things you wouldn't normally think about as a mom, but even as a tiny baby Gunner Lake just kind of knew the things he needed to do to help his mama. Like when LeAnn would change his diapers, he knew how to roll to make it easier for her, or if she was trying to carry him from room to room when he got a little older, he would know to push down on the door handle to help her open the door. Just little things like that. It's like he knew inside that he needed to help mama."

To make our house a whole lot easier for me to maneuver around with a baby we put flip door knobs on all our house doors. In fact, Gunner Lake even started opening the doors for me if he was in my arm—he would hang on me like a baby koala bear. His personality is a lot like mine; he's silly, he's an overachiever, and he has a heart of gold. I remember when he was small if someone tried to get him to play patty cake he would look at them like they were crazy. After all, that was one thing I couldn't teach him.

When Jeremy went back to work right after Gunner Lake came home from the hospital, my mom, aunts, and Jeremy's family helped out a lot. I didn't go places by myself, and if I absolutely had to go somewhere, Dana would come along. I hated to ask for help so it was comforting that I never even had to; it was so automatic with my family and friends and for that I'm humbled and thankful. No matter the occasion, family and friends were there to lend a hand, even during football season.

Alabama football is practically a state religion and that means game day is everything! You're either tailgating or having a watch party and having a baby to tote around with one arm made it a bit more challenging, but I felt the most comfortable going to game day events with my cousin Dana and her husband Clint. They made it possible to enjoy game days to the fullest.

I certainly have to mention my best friend Miranda and her parents who were my "out to eat" companions and they also helped me with shopping. Miranda's parents were as caring and kind as my own parents and I have always appreciated them.

Having one arm certainly didn't slow me down playing softball and it didn't slow me down as a mother either, although my husband, and my family and friends made it all that much better.

As of this writing, Gunner Lake is seven years old and just started second grade at a local private school. He used to attend a public school but we felt the need to switch him to a private school for more personalized instruction. And, as always, starting at a new school can be a bit daunting, especially for Jeremy and me. We had to ask ourselves, "Did we do the right thing? Will Gunner Lake make friends?" I have to admit that one of my biggest fears is Gunner Lake getting picked on because his mother has one arm. One good thing is at his new private school some of the teachers either played softball against me or with me so they know who I am. It helps knowing the teachers would do their best to explain the situation to the students if an issue like that ever came up.

As far as softball goes, I look forward to the day when I can pass on to Gunner Lake my love of playing ball and the life lessons I learned from it. That's what sports is all about—helping create a strong foundation for the type of person you will become later in life. I'm really hoping Gunner Lake will love playing sports as much as I did. It's already evident that he's an athlete. He loves football and we're hoping next year he can start flag football— it's all he talks about! He's actually crazy about three sports: football, baseball, and golf. At his school now, the kids get to order their football jerseys with their name and the number they want on it. Gunner Lake chose #8, my softball number. He's so excited about getting it and wearing his mom's number!

Parenthood has strengthened me in ways I cannot even explain. The word *can't* is still not even remotely a part of my vocabulary as I tend to motherhood with the same gusto I invested in softball. Parenting with one arm can be challenging but I never met a challenge I didn't overcome.

6th Inning

A Slice of Heaven and Bethany's Wave

On November 23, 2015, a phone call from one of my mentors in sports changed my life forever. Heaven Harris was 13 years old when a disastrous ATV accident caused her right arm to be severely crushed, ultimately resulting in amputation.

Heaven grew up playing softball in the Alabama Dixie Softball program. She was an extremely powerful right- handed pitcher, first baseman and hitter for the Ponytails X-Play team. She was in seventh grade playing against varsity, 18-year-old girls and already had college recruiters and coaches looking at her. She pitched really fast; 70-mile-per-hour balls. People who saw her play couldn't believe she was only 13 years old.

Heaven isn't the most common name so you may be wondering how she got her name; I mean you really don't hear that name very much. Her mom Brittney explains, "I thought I was having a boy until my last two-week check-up. The doctor was checking the baby's measurements and he said something like, 'are you ready for her to come out?' I was like, 'what…wait…what do you mean *her*? I just bought everything for a boy, including a bed, room accessories… everything.' My sister had wanted a girl and she had found out that very same day that she was having a boy and she had been buying girl stuff. We did a quick swap of everything we had bought so it wasn't too terribly complicated. I had already picked out boy names so we had to go back to the drawing board. My sister and I had gone to a boutique to find our baby's coming home outfits since we were due a couple months apart and there was a little girl in there and her mom kept saying 'come here Heaven.' My sister was like 'that's it, that's the name, Heaven. You've got to name her Heaven.' Thus, Heaven Marie Harris."

Much like the day of my accident, Heaven's day started out pretty normal; nothing out of the ordinary was happening. No one in her family had any reason to believe that their lives were about to change forever. They were all just going about their business.

Brittney recalls that fateful day when Heaven lost her arm:

> *My husband David and I had to go to the dentist with our son Hunter because he was having some dental work done and had an innate fear of the dentist. We were in the midst of trying to get him to stop crying while at the same time dealing with the rude, impatient dentist so I was already feeling aggravated.*
>
> *Heaven and her sisters Maggie and Mallison didn't want to come with us so they had a friend over and they wanted to stay at the house but I wouldn't let them because I didn't want the kids there by themselves. They decided they wanted to go to Heaven's best girlfriend Jessie's house. I told them 'same rules like when you're here—while*

we're gone you don't leave Jessie's house, you don't go outside.' The whole third-degree spiel we parents deliver. Well, a boy came over who they knew from school; he was on an ATV and he wanted them to go ride and of course they went. Later on the kids said that he was riding very recklessly. Even a lady who works at a local bank passed them on the road as she was going home for lunch and she told a friend of mine 'Oh God somebody's going to get hurt on that thing.' This kid riding the ATV and Heaven riding shotgun sped up the road which has a curvy bend and a hill, and then turned around to come back. There was a car coming which made him whip it to the left and they hit gravel so the ATV started to tip onto two wheels. As it started going over on Heaven's side, her first instinct she said was to stick her arm out and catch herself; the doctor relayed to us later that in doing so she probably crushed everything in her arm anyway. The ATV bounced back over and the bar on top of it landed on her arm and busted the artery.

So while all this was happening my husband and I were still at the dentist and I could see that my sister had called me several times but I didn't pick up her calls because of trying to calm my son down. Then my brother-in-law called and at that point I told my husband, 'I'm going to go outside and call them back because for them to call multiple times, something's wrong.' I called my sister back first and through a shaky voice, she told me, 'Brittney, Heaven was in an accident and she hurt her arm. She's at the hospital.' I said, 'Well, what are the doctors going to do?' She said, 'They're going to have to fly her to Birmingham.

It's bad, Brittney, and when I tell you it's bad, it's bad.' At this point I was thinking it's badly bruised or badly cut...or something like that.

My brother-in-law works about two miles from where the accident happened so the friends Heaven was with called him first. He left work immediately and came straight home. The ambulance was on their way to get Heaven but they had been delayed by a passing slow-moving train so it was taking them longer to get to her. My brother-in-law drove to the accident site, threw Heaven in the car, and raced her to Coosa Valley Medical Center. By the time I called *my sister back, they were already at the hospital.*

Heaven's Godmother, Dawn, had called me from the hospital too. She sobbed, 'It's so bad Brittany, it's so bad! They're coming to get her right now; they're flying her to UAB and they want to do surgery on her immediately.' I said, 'Okay, we're on our way.' I went back to the area where my son and husband were and told my husband, 'Let's go, we've got to go NOW!' The three of us dashed out the door and I can say my son was probably relieved he didn't have to go all the way through with the dental procedure that day. I drove because my husband is a very slow driver, although I swear I cannot remember driving—I don't even know how we made it to the hospital in Birmingham, but we did.

There was road construction on the interstate which made me even more aggravated. I remember at one point calling a friend who lives in Birmingham so she could detour us around the bumper-to-bumper traffic. I felt like we were never going to get there; it was like one of those dreams where everything seems to be moving in slow motion. All I wanted to do was get to UAB to see Heaven before she went into surgery.

We arrived right after the helicopter landed and I was able to see her for just a few minutes although I really couldn't see the extent of the damage to her arm so I still didn't know how really bad it was. At that point, the doctors didn't know either. They didn't mention anything about the possibility of amputation; they just told me that her arm was severely damaged and they had to go in to see what they were working with and stop the bleeding, which was their main concern because she was bleeding out so bad.

I was still thinking at that point that they might have to put a pin, a rod, screws, or staples in her arm to fix it up. The surgeon came out after the surgery and delivered the news: he said the artery in Heaven's arm was so severely damaged that their only option was to amputate. He said that if they didn't do it she would have no blood flow or feeling in her arm whatsoever, and that could set up an environment for infections. An infection meant that Heaven would need to be in and out of the hospital, and ultimately she would have to have her arm amputated anyway because of so much infection. He said an infection could be so bad that it could actually kill her if it got into her bloodstream.

When the staff let us into her room, Heaven was awake yet very groggy from the anesthesia. I leaned over her. 'Are you okay?' She sleepily replied, 'Yeah, my arm just hurts and it's strapped down.' It was like she wanted to tell me what happened but I told her, 'Don't tell me what happened, it's okay.' I didn't want to upset her. She kept telling me, 'I'm sorry, I'm sorry.'

The nurse told us that we would have to tell Heaven her arm was gone while she was in the recovery room because they didn't want her to try to roll on the bed and it not be there. The nurse said, 'I'm not rushing you but we do have to tell her before we take her up to her room because when we move her from bed to bed we don't want her to lean on that arm and discover it's not there.' So when she was fully awake we told her the news and the first thing out of her mouth was, 'How am I going to play ball?' followed quickly by 'I'm going to still play ball!' I responded, 'Yes, you can.' I said, 'You can do whatever you put your mind to.' That same day her coach talked to her on the phone and then brought her bat bag to her room. She would get up and swing that bat over and over with her other arm in the hospital.

They told us at the hospital that she would be in the rehab for something like two weeks afterwards so she could learn to do basic tasks one-handed. She also had to have several follow-up surgeries so they could go in and clean up the scar tissue. The physical therapist came in Heaven's room on the first day and said she had to be wearing socks for her therapy time. I handed Heaven her socks, and I felt his wondering stare; well God, you're her mom, are you just going to just sit there and make her put on her socks? But I knew my daughter. Heaven was independent and wanted to do things for herself. So she put her socks on, she got up and he took her out in the hallway. He came back after a short time to where I was waiting in her room and told me, "I'm sorry, ma'am but she doesn't qualify for rehab." I just looked at him and said, "What?" He replied, "No, it's a good thing. She doesn't qualify because she can do everything on her own. She didn't have a problem with balance or walking. Most of the time when people have accidents like that, even a week after, they're still having someone feed them. They're just down and won't try to do anything with one arm or whatever the case may be." I had always taught Heaven that she could do anything and she was certainly proving that to be true.

The entire time she was in the hospital Heaven held the idea that she was still going to play ball, regardless. Every time she mentioned it, I told her, 'Yes you can, I know you can!' I had seen videos of people who could play ball with one arm and I had always instilled in her the fact that she could do anything she put her mind to.

The first time LeAnn and her mom came it was about four or five days after Heaven got home from the hospital. I asked her to help Heaven learn basic tasks but playing ball wasn't even on my mind. I knew LeAnn played ball because I had talked to her on Facebook. I remember LeAnn brought her an electric can opener and told her she had one just like it; she showed her how it worked and also taught her other adaptation tricks for the kitchen and life in general. I let Heaven ask her about tasks she wanted to figure out how to do on her own.

As Brittney said, my mom and I traveled down to Sylacauga, Alabama about four or five days after Heaven came home to encourage her, and most of all to train her to adapt to playing softball with one arm. Our friendship grew, the more time we spent together. Jeremy, Gunner, and I traveled to Sylacauga for Heaven's multiple follow-up surgeries—I had been through the same ordeal and I knew what it was like. I showed Heaven how to accomplish certain tasks with one arm. There were certain things that took a special touch and the right tools to get it done.

"Heaven was right-handed and that's the arm she lost," says Brittney, "so she had to learn to do *everything* left-handed. Someone might pitch with their left hand but they don't throw with their left hand. She had to learn, just like LeAnn, to catch the ball, drop the glove, and throw the ball. She, of course, had to learn to write left-handed."

The first time we went over to her regular ballfield about a mile up the road, Heaven didn't really do much with the ball, she simply watched me pitch and hit the ball. When she saw me knocking the fire out of the ball, her face lit up. A local coach let us use a gym so we'd spend several hours working on fundamentals and drills.

Brittney says, "Heaven was like 'I want to do that, I want to play ball!' After a couple of months, we drove up and stayed three or four days with LeAnn, and they played all day long at a local church that had a field. They played all day long in that church field, throwing the ball and hitting the ball; they had the best time. One year both of our families were honored at a local church program for our accomplishments. The program was aptly named *Attitude is Everything*.

Living life with one arm, even for overcomers like Heaven and me, has its downside at times. Brittney relays the verbal cruelty that some ignorant people have spewed at Heaven.

"Heaven is a senior in high school and one of the things she has encountered is soon as somebody gets in an argument with her, the first thing they want to holler is 'you one-armed thing' or something equally as cruel. I think that bothers her to an extent but she doesn't let it show. She holds everything in. She had a job at Popeye's at the beginning of this year; she worked there for a couple of months. She worked the drive-thru and a few adults would get mad because they had to wait on their chicken, and they would say hateful things to her when they got to the window. It's bad enough when a kid or teenager says something hateful but when an adult does it, that just burns me up. I asked Heaven if she said anything back when one male drive-thru customer said something particularly hurtful and she said, 'I didn't say anything, I just looked at him.' She recently told me a couple of weeks ago that some girl started texting her and was calling her ugly names like one-armed this and that and Heaven was showing me the messages. She texted this young girl back, 'I know that, tell me something I don't know.' She seems to blow it off but I think it gets to her every once in a while."

Even amidst some of the cruelty, Heaven and I manage to maintain our humorous side. Since I had lost my left arm and Heaven her right, we would go together to get a manicure and each request half off. We loved watching the faces of the salon staff.

We have shared the ball field several times, and I was thrilled when Heaven got to pitch the first ball at one of the University of Alabama softball games.

Heaven has already been an inspiration to many. One of the kids at her school that had already graduated lost some of his arm when a firework blew up in his hand.

His sister called Heaven and told her, "My brother is so down and feeling ashamed. If anybody can help him Heaven, it's you because you have the best spirit when it comes to that." The girl continued, "I need you to talk my brother through this and tell him he will be able to keep going. He may have lost a hand but you've lost a whole arm."

I believe Heaven was able to talk to her brother although I don't know what happened to him after that.

A lot of people look up to Heaven—even older people. A lot of elderly people have told Heaven's mom, "I'm just so proud of her and when I get down on myself I just think of her because she's always got a smile on her face… always."

I told a newspaper reporter one time, "I've gone 30 years without a left arm and it took me 30 more years to find out my reason…"

Bethany's Wave

Several years before Heaven's accident, I had the joy and privilege of offering encouragement and support to Bethany Hamilton. She was 13 years old at the time and had been surfing off the coast of Kauai when she was attacked by a tiger shark that ripped off her left arm. The story made news around the world but I knew what she was going through on a very personal level and I wanted to help in some way. My purpose was playing out and I wanted to embrace the opportunity.

When I heard about Bethany I called Information and since I had her parents' names, I asked for the number. My call went to voicemail and it sounded like an attorney's office or something like that so I left a message, never expecting to hear anything back.

About a week later I got a call from Bethany's mother, Cheri. I encouraged her and told her that Bethany could and would overcome her new reality. I talked to Bethany too and I sent her all my articles to encourage her and show her anything was possible. She wrote a book about her life, and a movie with the same name, Soul Surfer, was made about her coming back to the surfing world after her recovery. Bethany has proved that comebacks are indeed sweet...and a lot of hard work!

Like me, Bethany's family is a wonderful supporting cast. Here is a short excerpt from a beautiful letter Bethany's mom sent me:

> *Thank you for your friendship. We like working out and keeping healthy with lots of vegetables and smoothies and when we're tired and grumpy we take a large spoonful of liquid B-complex and within an hour we are new people. Bethany and I spend a lot of time praying as we desire for the world to know the goodness and riches of God's love. We pray that God will give you great wisdom in helping people.*

Like Heaven and me, Bethany possessed a great sense of humor about her missing limb. While she was still in the hospital, her brother had brought home a realistic-looking fake foot from one of his trips to Mexico and she asked him to bring it to her. She stuck it under the bed and when one of the nurses came in Bethany exclaimed that there was something wrong with her foot. The nurse, looking concerned, reached under the sheets to check it out and practically jumped out of her skin when she felt the cold, rubber foot. Also like me, Bethany tried a prosthetic arm but found it too cumbersome and restricting. She calls what's left of her arm "stumpy." When you can maintain a sense of humor, it helps you *and* the people around you deal with everything a little bit better. Bethany sums it all up in her book[3], "Look, lots of bad stuff happens to people. That's life. And here's my advice: don't put all your hope and faith into something that could suddenly and easily disappear."

---

[3] Hamilton, Bethany, Soul Surfer, New York City: Pocket Books, 2004. Pg. 206.

7th Inning

What Part Are YOU Missing?

To know that the struggles and obstacles and pain I have faced and overcome could one day change another person's life or cause a parent to realize they need to love their kids and family like there's no tomorrow, makes it all worth it. The very act of overcoming requires faith—and faith is powerful. To me, faith is like softball. Your faith in God must be real and you should be able to throw it and most of all catch it. Faith has given me an avenue to express my competitive spirit but above all it has allowed me to be *just like everyone else*.

Now don't get me wrong—I'm no Pollyanna—I've had my moments of despair, and people have let me down along the way, but my handicap has never hindered me in accomplishing what I started. It might take longer and you will see devices I have used to improvise to get the job done, but don't tell me I can't do the job. Just give me a chance to show you I can do it.

My life is no fairy tale but God has bountifully blessed me beyond measure with a purpose and surrounded me with a loving family and friends. I live in a beautiful home encircled by nature but my greatest gifts are my husband Jeremy and our son Gunner Lake.

No matter what your circumstance, I encourage you to add some humor to your life! One time when I was playing softball, a teammate remarked before a game that they were going to be short-handed. I told her as I chuckled, "It's okay, I'm short-handed every day."

People are often surprised by the humor I direct at myself but I find it much better to laugh than anything else. I tell people, "Your faith will outlast the pain and grief you feel sometimes. Even though my situation is permanent, that doesn't mean I have to throw my hand up and give up!"

Through God anything is possible! I'm far from perfect but I know I'm forgiven so I can have peace every single day. You can too. No matter what you're facing, God can turn it around just like that. Our purpose for disappointment is where we find God's appointment for something better. God is a pretty good catcher so no matter what life pitches at you, He will catch it in His mighty and strong hands.

Is there a missing piece your life today, a broken area? Maybe there are several missing, broken pieces. Joni Eareckson Tada, who broke her neck in a diving accident when she was 17, her spinal cord severed, became paralyzed from the shoulders down. She became a renowned artist using her teeth to hold paint brushes and pencils. In 1993 Joni wrote a beautiful piece, *Shattered Glass*, as the May 8th entry in *Diamonds in the Dust: 366 Sparkling Devotions*[4]. I've included short excerpts here:

> *"Recently while cleaning up [my art studio], I discovered some broken glass by the window. I also discovered that when sunlight struck the shattered glass, brilliant, colorful rays scattered everywhere.*

---

[4] *Diamonds in the Dust: 366 Sparkling Devotions* by Joni Eareckson Tada Copyright © 1993. Excerpts used by fair use permission of Zondervan. www.zondervan.com

> *"What's true of shattered glass is true of a broken life. Shattered dreams. A heart full of fissures. Hopes that are splintered. But given time and prayer, such a person's life can shine more brightly than if the brokenness had never happened.*
>
> *"Only our great God can reach down into brokenness and produce something beautiful. Every broken dream and heart that hurts can be redeemed by His loving touch. God has in mind a kaleidoscope through which His light can shine more brilliantly."*

Will you allow God to pick up the shattered pieces of your life today? Will you allow Him to make you new again? All you have to do is ask! Ask Him to come into your heart and live there. He is ready to heal and restore your shattered pieces and your missing parts and your wounded places.

In many ways, my story is the story of millions of people around the world who have lost something in their lives; maybe you haven't lost a limb, or maybe you have. I know people who have lost arms, legs, or all four limbs.

Perhaps you've lost a loved one or maybe a beloved pet or your hopes and dreams. Maybe you've lost a love relationship you thought would last forever.

Maybe you've lost your health or your finances or your business or something else you once counted as near and dear to you. But now that thing or person is gone, and here you are facing your new reality and it's scary and daunting.

I want to challenge you with this thought: If God can "catch" my obstacles in life with His strong hands and turn them for good, He can also pick up your broken heart or broken life. When God's creation is broken, He is more than able and willing to fix it. He often asked broken people in the Bible if they wanted to be made whole. All they had to do was answer, "Yes, I want to."

I know it can seem hopeless at times. I understand how frustrating it can be to learn to live with a new permanent reality.

Whatever your loss, you must come to a point where you decide exactly *how* you're going to deal with that loss. Will you wallow in self-pity, forever wondering,

"Why me?" Will you become angry at the world for taking something from you? Will you become perpetually frustrated because you can no longer function the way you used to? Will you squirm with envy toward others who still have the piece you're missing? Will you doubt the sovereignty of God, and blame Him for your loss?

OR, will you square your shoulders, hold your head up and face your loss head on? Will you find ways you can excel in your circumstance? Will you encourage others who have experienced loss and tell them there IS hope, there IS life after loss? I hope and pray you choose the latter.

Now I'm not saying here that you won't go through a period of grief. Losing a limb is a loss of part of your physical self and the five stages of grief apply as they do with loss of a life.

And the grief process is not some systematic step system that comes in a neat and tidy package like okay, I'm on step two now, let's move on to step three. No! It takes time and it's quite all right if you need to enlist the help of a professional counselor if you find yourself staying stuck in one of the first four areas (denial/isolation, anger, bargaining, depression and finally, acceptance and hope). Recognize that there is a difference between normal, healthy grief and depression.

Since I lost my arm when I was four, I didn't experience some of the more grown-up emotions from losing a limb later on in life but I did experience feeling uncomfortable when I first went to school with my prosthetic arm. I did grieve as only a child can grieve but even as a child I never felt sorry for myself. I never even considered that I couldn't do certain things, especially play softball, because I chose to adapt. It all comes down to choice and every day we wake up we have a choice to either stay stuck or move forward. What will *your* choice be?

Dana was recently asked what she would tell me if we were face to face. She answered, "I would tell LeAnn what an amazing person she is and that she has more of an impact on people than she thinks she does; her inspiration from all she's been through, what she's overcome, and the things she has accomplished. It probably comes natural to her, but her example makes everybody else want to do better. She's just amazing." I'm humbled and grateful for Dana's words and they bring me to my next point.

It's crucial to surround yourself with positive, supportive people! I'm thankful that I had my family, friends, and coaches who stood by me. Seek out people who will do the same for you and avoid the negative ninnies like the plague.

Learn to focus on the positive aspects of your life. Maybe you're a great cook or a good friend, or funny, or a kind encourager.

Continue to be who you are!

Resist the urge to isolate yourself. Reach out for help when you need to. Others do not know exactly what you are going through but give them a chance—talking about your needs may help both you and those around you. Search for local or online support groups as it can be helpful to talk to someone else who has had a limb loss or some other major life loss. Those who have been where you are can offer experienced, empathetic advice. Don't rule out professional therapy if you feel you could benefit from it.

Exercise in a way that works for you. The benefits of exercise go beyond the physical realm. Regular exercise can elevate your mental health by helping to ease stress, anxiety, and depression. Support yourself emotionally by taking care of yourself physically.

Work hard to find your sense of self and your purpose for that will make you whole.

Wholeness is waking up to each new day knowing there are people in the world you care about, and a fresh set of chances to show them just how much. Wholeness is waking up knowing there are people who care about you as you feel their nurturing and love around every corner. Wholeness is the ability to see ourselves truthfully and accept our limitations as well as our areas of personal excellence. Wholeness rests in who and where we are in life, imperfections and all. The red stitches in a softball helped make me whole but really, it was the realization that wholeness does not depend on circumstances or emotion but rather a state of mind. Wholeness must be realized and received—it is a gift of God, and free of cost to anyone who asks.

"And we know that God causes all things to work together for good to those who love Him and who are called according to His purpose."

Romans 8:28

About the Author

"I am fearfully and wonderfully made, created in the image of God."

Psalm 139:14

LeAnn Sanders Shelton does not know how to say the word "can't." She also doesn't understand the meaning of the word "can't." That's because she's got positive purpose and a resolve to conquer any challenge that presents itself to her.

While in high school, LeAnn served as a Teacher's Assistant and Tutor for younger students in reading while at the same time earning her varsity letter as a member of Pickens County High School's softball team, the Lady Tornadoes. In 2000 she was voted team captain and in 2001 she was awarded the Most Valuable Outfielder.

With a 4.0 GPA, LeAnn graduated from Shelton State Community College in 2002 with a degree in Social Gerontology while completing 200 clinical hours in physical therapy.

After graduating college LeAnn was recognized by the Alabama Amateur Athletic Association, Birmingham Amateur Athletic Association, and Pickens County Herald Diamond Dozen. She is also a member of the Fellowship of Christian Athletes.

In 2018 LeAnn was featured in Tuscaloosa Magazine as one of six Intriguing People in Alabama. She received a national softball honor in 2015 by the Dixie Softball National Board of Directors when they named an award The LeAnn Sanders Shelton Courage Award. In 2013 LeAnn was inducted into the Dixie Softball Hall of Fame and also presented with a State of Alabama House of Representatives Resolution from John Merrill.

Through the years, LeAnn has served as an Optometrist Assistant and Physical Therapist Tech but her greatest and most rewarding roles have been those of wife to Jeremy and mother to Gunner Lake.

LeAnn states her mission boldly. "My ultimate goal is to be a lighthouse for others facing obstacles in life. I want to be their light of hope, faith, and courage for overcoming the impossible."

Acknowledgements

I'd like to thank the following family and extended family members for their loving support and encouragement all these years:

Family

-Jeremy Shelton, Gunner Lake Shelton

-James Sanders, Deborah Sanders

-Bobby Sanders, Tyler Sanders, Brittany Sanders, Levi Sanders

-Dale Shelton, Donna Shelton

-Mike Brown, Wendy Brown, Savannah Brown, Luke Brown

-Andrew Irvin, Brandy Irvin, Dylan Irvin

-John Hildreth, Wanda Hildreth

-Miranda Porter, Zeke Porter and Cade Owens, Ella Owens

-J.C. Hildreth, Rebecca Hildreth, Sophia Hildreth

-Dana Moorhead, Clint Kyles, Preslee Kyles

-Danny Moorhead, Dean Moorhead

-Larry Shelton, Donna Shelton

-Vaudine Lancaster and Family

-The Connell Family

-The Pate Family

-The Guy Family

-Pam Spurgin

Close Friends

-David Hill, Brittney Hill, Maggie Hill, Hunter Harris, Heaven Harris, Mallison Harris

-Dawn Collins

- Obie Evans

- Alabama Dixie Softball

- Shelby Lowe

- The Gurganus Family

- Joan Boothe

- Barbara Jordan and the late J.E. Jordan DVM

- Margie Duckworth and the late POP

- Ann Taylor

- Debbie Keasler Ballard

- Kitty Tilley

- The Dixon Family

- Natasha Conn and Family

- Dr. John Brandon

-The Brown Family

-The late Vicki Brown

-Becky Hopf

-Christy Keaton

-Laura Payne

-Wilma Renae Brown

-The late Libby Hankins #livelikelibbylovelikelibby

-The late Tanley Preston Adcock; 8-yr-old who passed away from an asthma attack

-The late Madison Orr

-Stone Turnipseed #STONESTRONG

-Bethany Hamilton (Dirks) and Family

-Rebecca (Noland) Richardson

-Parthenia (Tina) Oliver

-John Brooks (Lawn Mower Accident Support and Prevention) LMA Survivors & Family Support

-Amputee Coalition

-Pickens County Herald

-Sheri Faulk

-Lydia Hu

-Sandra Stripling

-Colton Woolbright

2001 Senior Class

-The late David (Spooky) Johnson

-The late Kera A Guyton

-The late Michael Plott

-The late Robin Spencer

-The late Josh Easter

-The late Jennifer Stough

-Keith Smith

-Chris McCrary

-Ashley (Petty) Burnley

-Valeria Spencer

-Jonathan Easterwood

-Alicia (Spencer) McGraw

-Katrina Williams

-Derrick Smith

Coaches

Thank you for seeing more in me, more than I thought I could ever be. Who taught me discipline. Who raised expectations and dreams, beyond just an athlete's schemes, beyond normal endurance, beyond myself, and ever since. I'm a greater person for it. Because you taught me not to quit.

-Lee Gibson

-Sandra Pemberton

-Lewis Grace

Teammates

Thank you for believing in me and never giving up on me. Also for the countless memories we made in our years together.

-Abby (Woodard) Myers

-Kim Taylor

-Jalynn (Abrams) Gray

-Jessica Hill

-Jade (Criswell) Maddox

-Angel Brown

-Robyn (Grace) Wilson

-Tera (Kelley) Glenn

-Lena (Bass) Lovelady

-Felicia Spencer

-Tiffany (Dixon) Prude

-Dana (Grace) O'Bryant

-Tiffine Daniels

-Tanya (Grace) Wilkins

-Cindy (Tunnell) Gann

-Lindsey Keasler

-Tara Bennett

-Becki (Fuller) Shaughnessy

-Brandy Hall

-Brandy (Prescott) Kernop

-Fran (Asher) Guerra

-Libby (Asher) Boone

-Heather Bryant

-Erin (Patton) Keasler

-Shanetta Giles

-Heather Kyzer

-The late Mandy Asher

-Sara (McBride) Craker

-Angie (Stripling) Junkin

-Alabama Dixie Softball Board Members

-Alabama Secretary of State John Merrill

Churches

I would like to express my sincere thanks for supporting me through my years:

-Hickory Grove Baptist Church

-Arbor Springs Baptist Church

-Ethelsville Baptist Church

-Mt. Moriah F.W.B. Church

-Union Hill Baptist Church

Teachers

Thank you for the impact you all made in my life. You all taught me how to exceed even my own expectations.

-Karla Bridges

-Ike Gipson

-Russ Wallace

-Susan Hankins Estes

-The late Ms. Martha Fuller

-The late Ms. Penny Henderson

-Glenda Pate

-Fernanda Storey Windham

-Bonnie Gammill

Special Mention

The late Tuscaloosa Police Department Investigator Dornell Cousette. You made a difference in our small town and your life mattered. I back the blue! Thank you for your service.

Thank you to Michelle Hill, *My Legacy Builder* at Winning Proof, and her team of professionals for helping to making this book a reality: Stacey Miner, transcriptionist; Michael LaRocca, proofreader; Michael Scott, cover design MASgraphicarts; Drew Becker of Affirmation Press, interior design and publisher.

How to Order

To <u>book</u> LeAnn Sanders Shelton for book signing events, to <u>order bulk copies</u>, or to <u>request media interviews</u>:

Email: redstitches88@gmail.com

This book can also be purchased both on Amazon and at barnesandnoble.com.

If you're a fan of this book, please tell others...

- Write about *Red Stitches* on your blog and social media channels.

- Suggest this book to your friends, family, neighbors, and coworkers.

- Write a positive review on Amazon.com.

- Purchase additional copies for your business or sports team, or to give away as gifts.

- Feature LeAnn on your radio or television broadcast.

www.ingramcontent.com/pod-product-compliance
Lightning Source LLC
Chambersburg PA
CBHW052135110526
44591CB00012B/1733